THE AMERICAN POLITY

THE AMERICAN POLITY: ESSAYS ON THE THEORY AND PRACTICE OF CONSTITUTIONAL GOVERNMENT

Edward J. Erler, Ph.D.
California State University
San Bernardino, California

CRANE RUSSAK
A member of the Taylor & Francis Group
New York • Philadelphia • Washington, DC • London

USA	Publishing Office:	Taylor & Francis New York Inc.
		79 Madison Ave., New York, NY 10016-7892
	Sales Office:	Taylor & Francis Inc.
		1900 Frost Road, Bristol, PA 19007-1598
UK		Taylor & Francis Ltd.
		4 John St., London WC1N 2ET

THE AMERICAN POLITY: Essays on the Theory and Practice of Constitutional Government

1 2 3 4 5 6 7 8 9 0   B R B R   9 8 7 6 5 4 3 2 1 0

Library of Congress Cataloging-in-Publication Data

Erler, Edward J.
   The American polity: essays on the theory and practice of
constitutional government / by Edward J. Erler.
       p.   cm
   Includes bibliographical references and index.
       1. United States—Constitutional history.   I. Title.
JK31.E75   1991
320.973—dc20   90-2666
                                                                                    CIP

ISBN 0-8448-1607-8 (case)
ISBN 0-8448-1608-6 (paper)

Contents

Introduction

Concern for constitutional government and its attendant political liberty is the unifying theme of the essays presented here. The apparent demise of Marxist governments in Eastern Europe and other parts of the world has provoked renewed interest in the principles and practices of constitutional government and the rule of law. The rule of law—the rule of reason—requires limited government because human reason itself is limited. It is this recognition of both the limits of politics and the limits of the human condition that furnishes the grounds for prudence in limited government. Prudence plays no role in Marxist-Leninist ideology because it recognizes no restraints on the human condition stemming from the principles of human nature. The reason is simple: what is called human nature is simply the result of the human organism's reaction to its environment. Human nature is therefore simply the by-product of the external forces of history and the organism's reaction to those forces. Human beings are what they are, not as a result of their nature, but as a result of their history. Change the environment—in Marx's case the abolition of private property—and human beings will become radically different beings. In Rousseau's phrase, human beings have an "almost unlimited faculty" for "self-perfection.'' In Marx's radicalization of Rousseau, the "almost unlimited" capacity became the unlimited capacity to reformulate human "nature." In Rousseau, history replaced nature as the distinguishing characteristic of human beings. But in Rousseau, the human capacity for self-perfection was premised on a radical human freedom. In Marx, however, this freedom is subordinated to an "iron law" of history—the historical material dialectic—in which there is neither nature nor freedom.

Much of the credit for the putative failure of Marxism-Leninism in Eastern Europe at least must be given to Alexander Solzhenitsyn's powerful revelations of the dehumanizing consequences of that ideology on the Soviet Union. In a statement that could have been made by Solzhenitsyn himself, a high-ranking party intellectual in the Soviet Union is reported to have said recently that "Marxism had misunderstood human nature and human motivations and consequently the political and economic systems founded on it are based on a false blueprint."[1]

Marxist-Leninists, unlike the founders of the American regime, maintain that human freedom, so far from being rooted in human nature, is merely a prescientific delusion. Freedom has no metaphysical reality; it is simply a "false-consciousness." Freedom has no independent existence as the cause of human behavior—it is merely the by-product or efflux of the material causes of existence. As Marx and Engels wrote in *The German Ideology,* "Conceiving, thinking, the mental intercourse of men, appear at this stage as the direct efflux of their material behavior. The same applies to mental production as expressed in the language of the politics, laws, morality, religion, metaphysics of a people."[2] Human beings—and their "nature"—are therefore simply the by-products of the historical-material-dialectic. Madison wrote that "The latent causes of faction are thus sown in the nature of man;" for Marxism-Leninism, however, it is private property—not man's nature—that creates "factions." Whereas Madison's vision of a just political order was limited by the fact that the causes of faction could never be eliminated, in the Marxist-Leninist vision, faction—and therefore political life simply—can be eliminated by the abolition of private property. "Human emancipation" thus will result from the annihilation of "egotistical man."

Any philosophy of human rights is simply a perpetuation of "egoism." "Liberty as a right of man," Marx writes, "is not founded upon the relations between man and man, but rather upon the separation of man from man. It is the right of such separation. The right of the *circumscribed* individual, withdrawn into himself."[3] Marx quotes with approval Rousseau's passage from the *Social Contract:* "Whoever dares undertake to establish a people's institutions must feel himself capable of *changing,* as it were, *human nature* itself, of *transforming* each individual who, in isolation, is a complete but solitary whole, into a *part* of something greater than himself, from which in a sense, he derives his life and his being."[4] But it must be remembered that in Rousseau's schema, along with the annihilation of the individual, by "substituting a partial and moral existence for the physical and independent existence we have all received from nature," it is necessary to force men "to be free."[5]

For Marxism-Leninism, morality—the choice of means—is merely the by-product or rationalization for existing class relationships and therefore only a transient feature of history. Any morality (or politics) that claims to be based on a permanent hierarchy of human ends is simply self-deluded and is replaced in Marx and Lenin by "historical consciousness," the belief that human beings have no nature and therefore no permanent ends. In the final synthesis of history, all human potential will be actualized. "In communist society," Marx and Engels wrote, "where nobody has one exclusive sphere of activity but each can become accomplished in any branch he wishes, society regulates the general production and thus makes it possible for me to do one thing to-day and another to-morrow, to hunt in the morning, fish in the afternoon, rear cattle in the evening, criticize after dinner, just as I have a mind, without ever becoming hunter, fisherman, shepherd or critic."[6] Without division of labor and its product, private property, the factions that "bourgeois theorists" believed were an intrinsic part of human nature will dissipate as will all false consciousness. When all human potential becomes actual, it is, of course, no longer necessary to choose or discriminate among the different potentials. Morality, which is now merely a means of conserving existing class relationships and therefore reactionary, will be superfluous in the final state.

Hannah Arendt once wrote that "all ideologies contain totalitarian elements."[7] The reason, Arendt indicates, is that ideology attempts to substitute history for nature or natural right as the animating principle of politics. Ideological regimes are thus prepared to sacrifice everyone's immediate interests to the dialectic of history, which dictates that every aspect of present existence is contradictory and only, at bottom, a *means* for a higher synthesis. Those who exist now "can only be executioners or victims of [the] inherent law [of history]. The process may decide that those who today eliminate races and individuals or the members of dying classes and decadent peoples are tomorrow those who must be sacrificed. What totalitarian rule needs to guide the behavior of its subjects is a preparation to fit each of them equally well for the role of executioner and the role of victim."[8]

Every ideology—indeed all modern thought[9]—has at its core the idea of "progressive" history. In Marxism-Leninism all history is a dialectic tending toward the final synthesis, which will be universal society of free and equal "species beings"—those having been transformed from egotists to communists. The final state will thus be the homogeneous world state. But seeing the present merely as a means to the future holds tremendous consequences for political action. From the progressive point of view, the present is always defective when seen from the perspective of the final state. For the present will never partake of the perfect or final character of the end to which it is a means.

History will inevitably be progressive since the present always serves, wittingly or unwittingly, as a dialectic for the final synthesis of all history.

The notion of progressive history is, I believe, the greatest cause of dehumanization that has ever existed. The belief that the historical dialectic can change not only the conditions of human existence but human nature as well inevitably makes all human beings who exist before the final synthesis of history appear radically defective or, one might say, inhuman. After all, such beings are only partly human (egotistical fragments of humanity) because a fully human life can exist only in the future communist state. Those who exist now bear the same resemblance to those who will exist in the future final state as an ape or a baboon to present-day "human" beings. This notion of history forces men to be partisan ideologues. Partisanship—one's attachment to ideological orthodoxy—is the only standard of humanness that remains in a universe in which all things are destined to pass into historical obscurity. Only partisans can regard one another as "human." And if the partisans, like everyone else, are alienated by the process of history from living a full existence, they can take comfort in the fact that they consciously play a part in the historical process that keeps them from attaining humanity—they serve in the vanguard.

This radical depreciation of the present, of seeing those who exist now merely as a means to some future, provides the great impetus for treating humans as if they were subhuman or partially human. And, of course, this dehumanization is a necessary prelude to the violence and terror that have been practiced with such vigor in the Soviet Union and other Marxist-Leninist regimes. Leo Strauss described the situation with characteristic precision:

> For some time, it appeared to many teachable Westerners—to say nothing of the unteachable ones—that Communism was only a parallel movement to the Western movement; as it were, a somewhat impatient, wild, wayward twin who was bound to become mature, patient and gentle . . . . For some time, it seemed sufficient to say that while the Western movement agrees with Communism regarding the goal of the universal prosperous society of free and equal men and women, it disagrees with it regarding the means. For Communism, the end, the common good of the whole human race, being the most sacred thing, justifies any means. Whatever contributes to the achievement of the most sacred end partakes of its sacredness and is, therefore, itself sacred.[10]

It was Solzhenitsyn who demonstrated with dramatic clarity the inherent connection between the principles of Marxism-Leninism and the dehumanizing violence and terror that became an integral part of Soviet rule. The Gulag is not some aberration of Stalin's but a necessary consequence of Marxism-Leninism's failure to recognize prudential limits on attempts to reform political life.

The kind of ideological dehumanization that is necessarily implied in progressivism is not possible under the natural right conception of human rights. As every reader of the Declaration of Independence knows, human rights—life, liberty, and pursuit of happiness—do not depend on history, but on the laws of nature and nature's God. The laws of nature and nature's God provide a non-historical insight into a permanent hierarchy of human ends. It is the abiding permanency of the laws of nature and nature's God, regardless of the character of the positive laws, that guarantees rights to human beings. Not connected to a theory of progressive history, the natural rights doctrine thus retains full consciousness of the distinction between means and ends; individual rights cannot be sacrificed now as a means to the fulfillment of some other future end. And it is this consciousness of the distinction between means and ends that forces the recognition of the limits of politics, of the prudential requirements that must mark the boundaries of any ordered and lawful regime. The consciousness of the limitations on political life—and the prudence and statesmanship necessitated by such consciousness—can be no part of the determined universe of Marxism-Leninism. The experience of the American founding is rooted in a recognition of the requirement and limits of human political nature. As Marxism-Leninism has proven, without such a recognition of human nature as the ground of political life, there are no limits to what can be claimed in the name of an ideology that looks forward to the final solution or the complete relief of the human estate.

An earlier version of Chapter One appeared in J. Jackson Barlow, Leonard W. Levy, and Ken Masugi, eds., *The American Founding: Essays on the Formation of the Constitution* (Westport, Conn.: Greenwood Press, 1988) and is reprinted with the permission of the Claremount Institute for the Study of Statesmanship and Political Philosophy; Chapter Three appeared in an earlier version in Leonard Levy and Dennis Mahoney, eds., *The Framing and Ratification of the Constitution* (New York: Macmillan, 1987) and is reprinted by permission of Macmillan Publishing Company, all rights reserved worldwide. Chapter Five is an extensively revised version of an article that appeared in 16 *Georgia Law Review* (1982) which was adapted with permission.

NOTES TO INTRODUCTION

1 Michael Parks, "For Delegates, the Key Question is 'Where Did We Go Wrong?' " *Los Angeles Times,* July 11, 1990, p. A 8, col. 1.

2 Karl Marx and Frederick Engels, *The German Ideology* (New York: International Publishers, 1947), p. 14.

3 "On the Jewish Question," in Robert C. Tucker, ed., *The Marx-Engels Reader,* 2nd ed. (New York: W. W. Norton, 1978), p. 42.

4 Ibid., p. 46.

5 Roger D. Masters, ed., *On the Social Contract* (New York: St. Martin's Press, 1978), pp. 68, 55.

6 *German Ideology,* p. 22.

7 *The Origins of Totalitarianism* (Cleveland: World Publishing, 1958), p. 470.

8 Ibid., p. 468.

9 Leo Strauss wrote that "Modern thought is in all its forms, directly or indirectly, determined by the idea of progress. This idea implies that the most elementary questions can be settled once and for all so that future generations can dispense with their further discussion, but can erect on the foundations once laid an ever-growing structure. In this way, the foundations are covered up. The only proof necessary to guarantee their solidity seems to be that the structure stands and grows." *What is Political Philosophy?* (New York: The Free Press, 1959), p. 6.

10 Leo Strauss, *The City and Man* (Chicago: Rand McNally, 1964), pp. 4–5.

Chapter One

Natural Right
in the American Founding

This is why we do not permit a man to rule, but the law, because a man rules in his own interest, and becomes a tyrant; but the ruler is a guardian of justice, and if of justice, then of equality.

—Aristotle, *Nicomachean Ethics*, 1134a35–1134b2

Do not destroy that immortal emblem of Humanity—the American Declaration of Independence.

—Abraham Lincoln, 1858

The Constitution's bicentennial in 1987 presented the natural occasion for reflection on the origins of the regime. Those who were closer to the origins understood better than we do today the primacy of first principles. In an early essay, "The Farmer Refuted," published in 1774, Alexander Hamilton wrote that "When the first principles of civil society are violated, and the rights of a whole people are invaded, the common forms of municipal law are not to be regarded. Men may then betake themselves to the law of nature; and, if they but conform their actions, to that standard, all cavils against them, betray either

1

ignorance or dishonesty."[1] This statement linking first principles of civil society to natural law was not merely the product of Hamilton's youthful enthusiasm.

In the same year, James Wilson argued in his "Considerations on the Nature and Extent of the Legislative Authority of the British Parliament" that "the most effectual method of perpetuating the liberties of a state" is to insure that the constitution is "frequently renewed, and drawn back, as it were, to its first principles."[2] Theophilus Parsons, in his highly influential *Essex Result,* published in 1778, expressed similar sentiments when he stated that "the want of fixed principles of government, and a stated regular recourse to them, have produced the dissolution of all states, whose constitutions have been transmitted to us by history."[3] This idea of a frequent recurrence to first principles also found expression in the Virginia Bill of Rights (1776) and the Massachusetts Bill of Rights (1780), both of which posit "a frequent recurrence to fundamental principles" as the indispensable means of preserving free government. In the closing days of the Constitutional Convention, Madison noted that the "people were in fact, the fountain of all power" and that they might resort to "first principles" in the alteration of constitutions. In response to Luther Martin's rejoinder that it was dangerous to "resort to the people and to first principles," Rufus King pointed out that Massachusetts—and by implication all the states— "must have contemplated a recurrence to first principles before they sent deputies to this Convention."[4]

America is unique. The American Founding represents the first time in human history that a people attempted to constitute itself by dedication to a principle—the principle that "all men are created equal" and its necessary concomitant that all legitimate government must be derived from "the consent of the governed." Tom Paine, the most powerful polemicist of the revolutionary period, wrote of America's uniqueness in the *Rights of Man:*

> The Independence of America, considered merely as a separation from England, would have been a mater but of little importance, had it not been accompanied by a revolution in the principles and practise of government. She made a stand, not for herself only, but for the world, and looked beyond the advantages herself could receive. . . . The revolutions which formerly took place in the world had nothing in them that interested the bulk of mankind. They extended only to a change of persons and measures, but not of principles, and rose or fell among the common transactions of the moment. What we now behold, may not improperly be called a *counter-revolution.*[5]

It may seem strange that Paine would characterize the American Revolution as a "counter-revolution." What he meant, however, is obvious. The America Revolution was unique. It was not a revolution that exchanged one set of rulers for another, but *contra* all revolutions that had heretofore transpired, it enshrined universal principle as the moving force of legitimate government. For the first time in history, reason or principle and not unfettered human will was to be the ultimate ground of political justice.

Perhaps no one—certainly no politician—has understood the character of the American Founding better than Abraham Lincoln, who, echoing Paine, wrote in 1859:

> All honor to Jefferson—to the man who, in the concrete pressure of a struggle for national independence by a single people, had the coolness, forecast, and capacity to introduce into a merely revolutionary document, an abstract truth, applicable to all men and all times, and so to embalm it there, that today and in all coming days, it shall be a rebuke and a stumbling block to the very harbingers of reappearing tyranny and oppression.[6]

As a "merely" revolutionary document, the Declaration, according to Lincoln, was unexceptional. What is truly exceptional is the fact that Jefferson sought to form the horizons of a particular political community from the "material" of the "abstract" or universal principle that "all men are created equal." This "abstract truth" is said, in the Declaration, to derive from "the laws of nature and nature's God." It was this derivation that led Paine, in the *American Crisis*, to write that the denial of the "natural right to independence" was a "kind of atheism against nature."[7] There can be little doubt that the Framers of the Constitution regarded the Declaration as supplying the principles of the Constitution. Madison in *The Federalist*, for example, noted that the Constitution embodied the "fundamental principles of the revolution" and was derived from "the transcendent law of nature and of nature's God."[8] Thus the Constitution, in Madison's view, must be properly read in the light of the principles of the Declaration. The self-conscious purpose of the Framers was to put those principles into motion through the instrument of constitutional government, a government that would have as its central purpose the equal protection of the laws understood as the equal protection of equal rights.

Today our most immediate access to regime principles is through the equal protection clause of the Fourteenth Amendment. Any consideration of equal protection ineluctably leads to a consideration of the principle of equality itself. And, if Chief Justice Rehnquist is correct—as I am convinced that he is—in characterizing the Supreme Court's equal protection decisions as "a series of conclusions unsupported by any central guiding principle,"[9] then we are presented with a matter of some urgency. There is little doubt that equal protection of the laws is the central tenet of constitutional government. Indeed, the framers of the Fourteenth Amendment often described their handiwork as declarative of the central principles of the Constitution itself.[10] All civil liberties are traceable to this basic constitutional precept. As a constitutional precept, equal protection derives its dignity from the fact that it is the conventional reflection of principles that flow directly from natural human equality. Most of those who debated the Fourteenth Amendment knew they were engaged in a far-ranging debate about the fundamental principles of the Constitution. Indeed, the Reconstruction amendments must be viewed, in some sense, as an attempt to complete the regime of the Founding.

The regime of the Founders was incomplete because it had allowed the continued existence of slavery. The Constitution was, therefore, an imperfect expression of those principles enunciated in the Declaration of Independence, particularly the injunction that the moving principle of legitimate government was the "consent of the governed." The incompleteness of the Constitution was, of course, dictated by political necessity. A more radical position on the question of slavery would surely have spelled the defeat of the Constitution. Under the pressing circumstances, the best the Founders could accomplish was to create an instrument of government that, although tolerating slavery, nevertheless put slavery on what Lincoln rightly termed "the road to ultimate extinction." Lincoln explained in June 1857 that the authors of the Declaration

> did not mean to assert the obvious untruth, that all men were then actually enjoying that equality, nor yet, that they were about to confer it immediately upon them. In fact they had no such power to confer such a boon. They meant to set up a standard maxim for free society, which should be familiar to all, and revered by all; constantly looked to, constantly labored for, and even though never perfectly attained, constantly approximated, and thereby constantly spreading and deepening its influence, and augmenting the happiness and value of life to all people of all colors everywhere.[11]

This view was the one that animated the debate in Congress over the passage of the Fourteenth Amendment. The remarks of Representative Newell before the House on February 15, 1866, are not atypical. He noted that the Declaration was the "living principle" of the Constitution that provided it with "meaning" and an "independence." Speaking of the Framers of the Constitution, Newell remarked that

> the combined wisdom of these patriotic men produced our present Constitution. It is a noble monument to their ability; but unfortunately, like all human instruments, it was imperfectly constructed, not because the theory was wrong, but because of the existence in the country of an institution so contrary to the genius of free government, and to the very principles upon which the Constitution itself was founded, that it was impossible to incorporate it into the organic law so that the latter could be preserved free from its contaminating influence.[12]

Newell agreed with Lincoln that the Framers of the Constitution had put slavery in the ultimate course of extinction. "The framers of the Constitution," he noted,

> did what they considered best under the circumstances. They made freedom the rule and slavery the exception in the organization of the Government. They declared in favor of the former in language the most emphatic and sublime in history,

while they placed the latter, as they fondly hoped, in a position favorable for ultimate extinction.[13]

But, as Newell duly noted, the fond hope of the Framers had not been realized; indeed, slavery had become the rule and freedom the exception after the Kansas-Nebraska Act and the *Dred Scott* decision. The Civil War, according to Newell, was fought to restore the Declaration to its rightful place as providing the authoritative principles of republican government.

> And so this Constitution of our fathers, because of the existence of an element foreign to its genius and principles, flatly subversive of the ideas on which it was founded, and which gave the lie direct to its declaration of rights, was in such danger of utter destruction that the patriotic people of the nation found themselves compelled to abandon it altogether as the aegis of their liberty and safety or take up arms in its defense.[14]

Thaddeus Stevens, the leading Radical Republican, made this exact same point in a speech urging adoption of the Fourteenth Amendment before the House on May 8, 1866:

> It cannot be denied that this terrible struggle sprang from the vicious principles incorporated into the institutions of our country. Our fathers had been compelled to postpone the principles of their great Declaration, and wait for their full establishment till a more propitious time. That time ought to be present now.[15]

These invocations of the Declaration as providing the guiding principles for the Fourteenth Amendment were by no means isolated ones.[16] Representative Miller, for example, stated in debate before the House on May 9, 1866, that the first section of the Fourteenth Amendment was "so clearly within the spirit of the Declaration of Independence of the 4th of July, 1776, that no member of this House can seriously object to it." Indeed, references to the Declaration as "organic law" were so frequent throughout the debates that it can hardly be doubted that the Reconstruction Congress was self-consciously engaged in an attempt to restore the Declaration as the authoritative statement of the principles of the regime.[17] As Thomas Grey has written,

> the natural-rights constitutional theory, built around the concepts of due process, of national citizenship and its rights, and of the human equality proclaimed in the Declaration of Independence . . . was the formative theory underlying the due process, equal protection, and privileges and immunities clauses of the 14th Amendment.[18]

This is hardly surprising since the debate over the Fourteenth Amendment took place within the political horizons that had been forged by Lincoln in his debates with Stephen Douglas.

Whatever ambiguities there may be concerning the intentions of the fram ers of the Fourteenth Amendment, it is clear that their principal purpose was to secure federal citizenship for the newly freed slaves and extend to them the whole panoply of civil rights that are the necessary incidents of federal citizenship. In order to forestall attacks upon the citizenship of the former slaves, the framers of the Fourteenth Amendment made federal citizenship primary and state citizenship derivative, so that any person who was a citizen of the United States was automatically a citizen of the state where he resided. This made it impossible for the states to circumvent federal protection for civil rights by withholding state citizenship from the former slaves and thus preventing them from becoming citizens of the United States. The rights attaching to federal citizenship were thus brought within the protection of the United States Congress. Whatever rights were extended to white citizens would be extended equally to blacks. This is the clear and indisputable meaning of the first section of the Fourteenth Amendment. Equal protection of the laws must thus be understood as the equal protection of equal rights. And in 1868 these rights were still described as "natural rights."[19]

It almost goes without saying that today the language of natural rights—to say nothing of the language of natural law—has fallen into desuetude. The idea of natural rights began to disappear from political discourse almost immediately after the adoption of the Reconstruction amendments. Lincoln's restoration of the Declaration as the "standard maxim" of the regime was short lived. Under the onslaught of historicism and positivism in its various guises—all originating in Continental thought—the idea of nature as a standard for political life became almost an anathema. The Founders themselves had stood in opposition to the powerful strands of historicism and positivism that were gaining currency in the late eighteenth century. The doctrines of Rousseau and Kant stood in explicit opposition to the natural law doctrine of the Founders.[20] But historicism and positivism—or more precisely a combination of the two—became powerful in America in the years after the Declaration of Independence, culminating most dramatically in Stephen Douglas's doctrine of squatter sovereignty, and Chief Justice Taney's decision in the *Dred Scott* case.

In its premise that slavery was merely a matter to be determined by the interests of local majorities, Douglas's doctrine of "squatter sovereignty" was a purely positivistic doctrine. There were no natural rights that belonged to slaves that could thwart the will of such majorities. But, as Lincoln pointed out, on purely positivistic terms there was no argument for enslaving blacks that could not also be used as an argument for enslaving whites. Human liberty must therefore find a ground that is independent of human will and caprice. Lincoln opposed Douglas by arguing that positivism could provide no *principle* of government. Lincoln urged the readoption of the Declaration as a reaffirmation of the principles of the regime, principles that Lincoln believed were ultimately derived from nature or natural right.[21] Yet it seems that the dictum that "justice is the interest of the stronger" is the most perdurable of all political postulates,

and will always have a greater share of adherents. Regimes based upon principle will always be the exception and will always be destined, it seems, to stand
in the maelstrom of positivism.[22]

It has been many years since the Supreme Court has taken seriously the
notion that rights might exist by nature.[23] Legal realism—the dominant jurispru-
dential philosophy of the Court in this century—has discredited the idea of
"nature" or "natural law." Justice Black wrote in 1947 that "the 'natural law'
formula . . . should be abandoned as an incongruous excrescence on our Constitution . . . [a] formula . . . [which is] itself a violation of our Constitution."[24]
What legal realism had taught Justice Black was that the language of natural law
is merely a sophisticated justification for the personal predilections of judges,
and therefore arbitrary from a legal point of view. The Constitution was to be
taken in its most literal sense as an expression of positive law, and not as
embodying principles that could ultimately be traced to nature. Here Justice
Black was merely reflecting the thought of Justice Holmes, the most articulate
and influential representative of legal positivism in the twentieth century. It
would almost belabor the obvious to point out that Black's view of "natural
law" has nothing in common with the view of the Founders. For the Founders,
natural law was the law of reason and thus the ground for the rule of law itself.
But Black's view is the one that prevails today. J. H. Ely, currently the foremost
expositor of the canons of constitutional interpretation, rejects both natural law
and reason as possible sources for interpreting the Constitution. Natural law,
Ely writes, is "so uselessly vague" that one is forced "to choose between
triviality and implausibility." Reason is said by Ely to be "inherently an empty
source" and thus liable to be merely identified with the "values of the 'reasoning class'." This renders the idea of reason as the basis of constitutional law
"so flagrantly elitist and undemocratic that it should be dismissed forthwith."[25]

This "reasoning" almost inevitably leads to the view that, in Michael Perry's words, "the Constitution consists of a complex of value judgments the
framers wrote into the text of the Constitution and *thereby* constitutionalized."[26]
Thus the Constitution is seen to be merely a document that embodies the "values" of those who wrote it; the fact that the Framers believed that their work
was informed by "the laws of nature and nature's God" must be dismissed as
the self-deception not only of the Framers, but of the age in which they lived.
Modern science, of course, teaches that it is impossible to derive "values' from
facts. From the point of view of positive science, values are merely subjective
preferences since there are no objectively valid measures of "value." This view
forms the theoretical basis of the legal realism that, in one form or another, has
dominated American jurisprudence in the twentieth century.

In more recent years some constitutional commentators have come to realize that the same reasons that led to the discrediting of natural law and natural
rights also necessitate the discrediting of the idea of equality, for equality implies or points to nature or the necessity of nature. Supporters of the modern

welfare state have somewhat belatedly come to realize that radical reform is much easier to promote if all notions of right are positive. When all notions of right are positive, there are no limits to what can be demanded in the name of welfare, especially when it is recalled that the modern technological state looks forward to the total relief of the human estate, a relief that necessarily entails a denial that nature can provide standards or bounds to the human political condition. Nature will have to be subjected to human willfulness, i.e., technology, if the modern welfare state is to become a reality. The way was prepared for a full-scale attack on the idea of equality when constitutional commentators began to speak a few years ago of equal protection as the "right to equal dignity and respect," rather than as the right to "equal protection of the laws."[27]

The background for this interpretation was furnished by John Rawls's *A Theory of Justice,* published in 1971. Indeed, debate concerning constitutionalism and the principles of distributive justice is dominated today by this seminal work. According to Rawls, the kind of liberalism represented by the Constitution—particularly the liberal notion of equal protection as equal opportunity—is unjust because it allows "social primary goods" to be apportioned on the basis of "unmerited" or "arbitrary" natural inequalities or, as Rawls terms it, "the outcome of [a] natural lottery . . . [which] is arbitrary from a moral perspective."[28] A "moral perspective" therefore seeks to "nullify the accidents of natural endowment."[29] Short of abolishing all natural differences by technological means (Rawls does make some suggestions, however, about the possibility of eugenics),[30] compensation for those "least favored" must be the political justification for the continued existence of "superior natural talent." Since nature apparently creates a condition of inequality, Rawls's notion of equality cannot be derived from nature; equality is a correction of nature and is purely conventional—one of "our considered judgments." But if our notions of equality are merely conventional, then there are no limits to the demands that can be made in the name of equality, including the demand for inequality.

We will not be so unjust as to ask Rawls how he knows nature to be "arbitrary." Arbitrariness itself is not an object of possible knowledge. To call something "arbitrary" implies that there is a nonarbitrary standard by which arbitrariness itself can be judged.[31] It is rather amazing, however, that Rawls maintains that nature "by lottery" has created some capacities that are "*superior.*" How does Rawls know they are superior? It is impossible to judge relations of superiority and inferiority in an arbitrary universe. Such relationships could not possibly exist. The closest Rawls ever comes to any elucidation of these matters is his assertion—without discussion as far as I can discern—of "a natural sense of justice" that resides in every human being!

The Founders of the American regime understood equality to be the distinguishing feature of human nature. Human beings possessed the same human rights because they were equally possessed of the same nature. The evidence of this equality was the most empirical fact of the human condition—that among the human species there were no natural rulers. James Wilson succinctly stated the accepted view of the matter in his lecture "On the Law of Nature":

> Between beings, who, in their nature, powers, and situation, are so perfectly equal, that nothing can be ascribed to one, which is not applicable to the other, there can be neither superiority nor dependence. With regard to such beings, no reason can be assigned, why any one should assume authority over others, which may not, with equal propriety, be assigned, why each of those others should assume authority over that one. To constitute superiority and dependence, there must be an essential difference of qualities, on which those relations may be founded.[32]

This statement was not intended to imply, however, that there were no natural inequalities among human beings, only that there are none that would make one individual the *natural* ruler of another. Natural inequalities that exist in the state of nature have no practical force, since conditions in the state of nature blunt all differences. It requires the establishment of civil society—and the establishment of civil rights—for any natural human inequalities to manifest themselves. Each individual in the state of nature is the sole proprietor of his life, liberty, and happiness. Natural rights thus adhere to the individual as a participant in a species that is characterized, above all, by its equality. Legitimate government can therefore proceed only from the unanimous consent of those who are to be governed and has as its sole legitimate object the protection of the antecedent and pre-political (natural) rights of those who have consented to be governed. The goal of civil society is to secure as equally as possible the natural rights of those who have voluntarily consented to become members of civil society. But the pursuit of these rights within the context of civil society leads to different results, and society can justly recognize and reward different abilities and efforts. It is the existence of differing natural abilities that provides the ultimate ground of civil liberties.

It hardly needs to be pointed out that the natural right of the American Founding is not classic natural right. To say nothing of other considerations, the classic political philosophers rejected egalitarian natural right. As Strauss explained it, "[t]he political problem consists in reconciling the requirement for wisdom with the requirement for consent. But whereas, from the point of view of egalitarian natural right, consent takes precedence over wisdom, from the point of view of classic natural right, wisdom takes precedence over consent."[33] In 1787 the classic solution was unavailable to the Framers. For whatever reasons—not the least of them being the advent of Christianity—egalitarian natural right was the only possible form of natural right to which the Framers could resort. But the true character of the natural right of the American Founding is not to be seen in a comparison with the classics, but in a comparison with the likes of John Rawls. And, in this crucial regard, it must be remembered that in Aristotle's account natural right is a part of political right which, although everywhere having the same force or power, is nevertheless changeable.[34] Among other things, Jefferson was still able to hope that a natural *aristoi* might command the suffrages of the people.

Generally speaking, in the American Founding period, the words "equality" and "liberty" were understood as virtually synonymous terms. Equality was most often described in the phrase "equal liberty." Since human beings are said to be equal by nature and therefore have no natural rulers, they are free to choose their form of government. Every other species has its form of social organization imposed upon it by nature or instinct. The queen bee, for example, is naturally the ruler of the beehive, having been marked out by natural superiorities for rule. The hierarchy of the beehive is imposed upon the hive by nature. Bees have no capacity to change this relationship and no consciousness that change is possible. There will never be a convention of bees that decides that the matriarchal rule of the queen bee is unjust and propose the dictatorship of the proletariat as an alternative. A similar relationship subsists among every other social species. The male dominant lion will always rule the lion pride, even though there may be disputes from time to time as to which male lion is dominant. Lion prides have always been ruled by dominant males and will always be so ruled. This form of rule is imposed upon the lions—and all other social animals—by natural instinct. Human beings, in contrast, have the potential to determine their form of rule because, among the human species, there are no natural rulers. In a much quoted passage from the last letter he wrote, Jefferson gave an explanation of the true ground of the Declaration's assertion that "all men are created equal." "The general spread of the light of science has already laid open to every view the palpable truth, that the mass of mankind has not been born with saddles on their backs, nor a favored few booted and spurred, ready to ride them legitimately, by the grace of God."[35] It is certainly true that "accident and force" are the usual determinants of the form of human political community, but it is true nonetheless that freedom to choose is a potential of human nature.

Human beings do not have the instincts for social organization that are manifest in every other species. The human mind is not determined in the same way that instinct determines all other beings. Human beings are capable of individual self-consciousness and, although members of a species, can see themselves as individuals within the species. It is this possibility of self-consciousness, the proof that the human mind is not determined, that is the ground of human liberty. Jefferson in his "Bill for Establishing Religious Freedom" wrote "that Almighty God hath created the mind free, and manifested his supreme will that free it shall remain by making it altogether insusceptible of restraint."[36] Thus religious liberty, in Jefferson's mind, was an irrefragable dictate of human nature—the liberty that is the necessary conclusion from the fact that the human mind is not determined. In his discussion of religious liberty, Jefferson also demonstrated that he understood the difference between natural rights and natural right when he wrote that "the rights hereby asserted [sc. those associated with the free exercise of religion] are of the natural rights of mankind, and that if any act shall be hereafter passed to repeal the present or to narrow its operation, such act will be an infringement of natural right."[37]

The regime that is grounded in natural right will thus have liberty as its end. This will entail the recognition of both the sameness and the diversity of human beings. The philosophic problem of the one and the many seems to be at the bottom of all attempts to understand natural right. All human beings are equally members of the species and have the equal rights that necessarily adhere to such membership, but each individual is uniquely situated with respect to the exercise of those rights. The principle of a just regime, therefore, will be "from everyone according to his capacity and to everyone according to his merits." We have come to know this principle as "equality of opportunity," a principle that accords every individual "the opportunity corresponding to his capacities, of deserving well of the whole and receiving the proper reward for his deserts."[38] As a practical proposition, the different abilities that exist in civil society are expressed most dramatically in terms of the right to property.[39] Everyone has an equal right to possess property, but all have different—even unique—faculties for its acquisition. In fact, without the diversity of faculties, property would be homogeneous and the right to property as an *exclusive* appropriation would be nonexistent. It is the individual diversity of faculties that makes property itself individual, that is, private. All property carries the mark of the unique ability (labor) of the one who creates the property. If the faculties for acquiring property were homogeneous, everyone would be entitled to equal property, but no one would have an exclusive right to any particular property since no property would bear the stamp of creativity that was the exclusive possession of any single individual. Without human individuality, the natural right to property that is shared equally by all because of each individual's participation in the human species could not be translated into a civil right. And without civil protection for the right to property, the right to property itself would be a nullity, for in the state of nature there would be no occasion for an individual to distinguish himself by labor or otherwise. The natural right to property, understood in this manner, provides both the principle of identity and difference. And this is true of the natural right to life and liberty as well. It is not so much one's equal participation in the species—or one's species beingness as it has been termed—but one's individuation within the species that is uniquely human.

The Framers of the American Constitution believed that the right to property was, at bottom, the foundation of all rights. Madison, for example, wrote in 1792 that "as a man is said to have a right to his property, he may be equally said to have a property in his rights."[40] Accordingly, Madison wrote in *The Federalist* that "the first object of government" was to protect "the diversity in the faculties of men from which the rights of property originate."[41] Madison continued that "From the protection of different and unequal faculties of acquiring property, the possession of different degrees and kinds of property immediately results: and from the influence of these on the sentiments and views of the respective proprietors, ensues a division of the society into different interests and parties."[41] The character of civil society is thus determined in great measure by the interests and parties generated by the distribution of property.

According to Madison's argument, the existence of diverse forms of property and diverse interests makes the development of rigid distinctions between classes less probable. The goal of the Founders was not to prevent all class distinctions based on property (this would be impossible in a free regime), but to prevent those class distinctions from becoming the sole basis of political life. In a word, their goal was to create a society that replaced the arbitrary system of class and caste that characterized feudal society with a system in which there would be no preordained class barriers to the development of *natural* talent. The protection of the natural diversity for acquiring property is at one and the same time an affirmation of the equality of the right to property and a legitimation of the possession of different kinds and amounts of property. The American Founders thus sought to replace historical prescription by natural rights precisely because the existence of natural rights does not depend on human will or convention. Whereas historical prescription is ultimately traceable to accident, the existence of natural rights can be demonstrated as a "self-evident truth" from the laws of nature and nature's God, the first principle of which is the natural equality of all human beings. It is this change from historical prescription to natural rights that represents the radical core of the American Revolution and the American Founding.

Equality points to nature because equality is the abiding characteristic of the human condition. Reflection on the natural human condition thus also points necessarily to the possibility of natural right, a possibility coincident with the human condition itself. If history supplies only the prescriptive basis for society, reason holds out the prospect of supplying the principled basis. The existence of tradition or prescription always makes it difficult to discern the possibility of natural right, for authority always attempts to obscure or obfuscate the idea of natural right. But natural right supplies the ground of authority that is older than the history or traditions of any political order or religion. Nature is the oldest and most venerable authority, because the uncreated *archai*—the first principles—furnish the objects of reason. And this idea was not entirely unknown to Colonial America. In 1764 James Otis wrote in his *The Rights of the British Colonies Asserted and Proved* that "the form of government is by *nature* and by *right* so far left to the *individuals* of each society, that they may alter it from a simple democracy or government of all over all, to any other form they please. Such alteration may and ought to be made by express compact . . . " For, Otis continues, "there can be no prescription old enough to supersede the law of nature, and the grant of God almighty; who has given to all men a natural right to be *free,* and they have it ordinarily in their power to make themselves so, if they please."[43] As Otis clearly implies, it is reflection on the first principles that reveals the ground of political life. And these principles were known to the Founding generation as the "laws of nature." And as I think some of the Founders must have known—or divined—natural law is the only access in the modern world to natural right.

For the Founding generation, a regime grounded in the "laws of nature and nature's God" promised to provide the foundation for the rule of law that was lacking in the *ancien regime.* There was surely no more inveterate hater of the *ancien regime* than Jefferson, who wrote of the Declaration of Independence on the occasion of its fiftieth anniversary:

> May it be to the world . . . the signal of arousing men to burst the chains under which monkish ignorance and superstition had persuaded them to bind themselves, and to assume the blessings and security of self government. That form which we have substituted, restores the free right to the unbounded exercise of reason and freedom of opinion.[44]

Reason, flowing from the laws of nature and nature's God, was to be the substitute for the capricious class and caste system of the *ancien regime,* for the laws of nature are here understood by Jefferson as the rational creature's participation in the eternal law. This was John Locke's understanding when he described the law of nature as the law of reason, for reason—Professor Ely to the contrary notwithstanding—is not the preserve of any class, and on this account provides the necessary foundation for republican self-government, the only form of government that Jefferson believed was "consistent . . . with natural right."[45]

Honors and rewards in the new order would be apportioned according to natural merit, not as in the old order according to the privileges of caste and class. This system would not partake of the capriciousness of the old order because the apportionment of natural talent does not depend on human will. And as the rule of law requires that no individual or class interest be represented in the law, this system of distributive justice holds the prospect of providing the solid ground for the rule of law. This is the correct gloss on the famous passage from the *Notes on the State of Virginia* where Jefferson queried, "can the liberties of a nation be thought secure when we have removed their only firm basis, a conviction in the minds of the people that these liberties are of the gift of God? That they are not to be violated but with his wrath?"[46] If the rights of individuals are ever thought to be the creation of government or to be enjoyed only at the sufferance of others—whether of other classes or races— then rights would never be secure. Rights understood as purely positive rights have no support other than the will of the authority that creates the rights. Their security rests, therefore, on the conviction that rights come from the hand of

God or exist by nature or nature's God. Any other conviction would subject the exercise of rights to the whim and will of human capriciousness, the ultimate resort of despots. The precocious Alexander Hamilton made this precise point in a passage criticizing Hobbes in "The Farmer Refuted": "Moral obligation, according to him, is derived from the introduction of civil society; and there is no virtue, but what is purely artificial, the mere contrivance of politicians, for the maintenance of social intercourse. But the reason he ran into this absurd and impious doctrine, was, that he disbelieved the existence of an intelligent superintending principle, who is the governor, and will be the final judge of the universe."[47] This superintending principle, Hamilton continued, is the foundation of the law of nature.

One might argue—as indeed Rawls does—that a system of distribution according to natural talent and ability only perpetuates the arbitrariness of nature, for, as we recall, it is Rawls's assertion that nature is a "lottery," dispensing superior talent capriciously. It is therefore unjust, Rawls claims, that those who are lucky in the lottery of nature should profit from their good fortune in civil society, because no one is responsible for his own superior talent. But Rawls's notion would make all just desert impossible, since no one is responsible for his own being. Michael Zuckert has written that

> liberal equality . . . may be perfectly willing to say men deserve differential reward for the exercise of differential natural endowment and effort; but, Rawls could say, liberal equality has merely failed to raise the question whether those bases are themselves deserved . . . We then either have an infinite regress of bases of desert or arrive at some basis, some beginning point, which the individual cannot claim to have deserved or to be responsible for, but only to have been given. After all, no human being exists *causa sui* . . . To demand, as Rawls does, that no just claim rest on an undeserved base simply means that we must cease speaking about justice, for on the basis of that demand there can never be any just claims—not even for equality.[48]

It is more than curious, however, that Rawls can denominate some talent as *naturally* "superior." If, as Rawls maintains, nature is arbitrary, he cannot possibly know that some talents are "superior." It can be said that the individual apportionment of talent is arbitrary only on the presumption that nature has a purpose against which the particular manifestations of nature are exhibited. The individuation within nature points to the necessity of understanding nature as purposeful.

Nature, it is true, seems to apportion talents and abilities to individual human beings in no immediately discernible pattern. Nature is no respecter of class or caste, as the frequent failure of talented parents or classes to produce talented sons and daughters testifies. But the recognition that some individuals are superior by nature points to an order of nature that allows us to judge superiority and inferiority, although there are no superiorities—whether of intel-

lect, beauty, or strength—that are sufficient to make anyone the natural ruler of
another. The important point about nature's distribution is that it is independent
of human will and convention, and that the individual is the recipient of unique
talents and abilities. Because this distribution does not depend on human will, it
provides the necessary ground for the rule of law, for whatever else the rule of
law may mean, it requires that principle or reason rather than human fiat be the
informing agent of the law. Without a ground in nature—or in some other
nonarbitrary principle that is discovered by human reason rather than created by
human will or convention—justice merely becomes the "interest of the
stronger," or one of "our considered judgments." One of the most revealing
indications that the Rawls system rests wholly upon convention is the fact that
he never mentions the right to revolution, nor does he ever indicate the necessity of deriving legitimate government from the consent of the governed.[49]

In the American political order the idea of equality—the principle of the
American Revolution—has always provided our access to nature and therefore
to natural right. And equality as an expression of nature necessarily means that
rights—natural rights—adhere to individuals, or are the exclusive possession of
individuals. But we are told by authoritative commentators today that equality
should be merely regarded "as the constitutional rhetoric of choice,"[50] or that it
"is an idea that should be banished from moral and legal discourse as an
explanatory norm." This last quote is from Peter Westen—an epigone of
Rawls's—who argues that rights should be understood independently of any
idea of equality. Rights, Westen maintains, are merely claims "made by or on
behalf of an individual or group of individuals to some condition or power. . . .
"[51] Rights are thus merely positive claims to entitlements or positions of power.
There are no limits either to what can be claimed as a right or as to what might
be claimed as the source of right. As Westen notes, "the right may be a 'liberty,' 'privilege,' 'power,' 'exemption,' or 'immunity,' [and] may have its source
in law or morals or custom; it may be comparative or noncomparative; it may
consist of a principle or a policy; it may be absolute or defeasible."[52] One must
necessarily wonder whether any argument for right can be effective that is not
ultimately grounded in the principle of natural human equality. To make right
depend on interest—as Stephen Douglas once attempted and Westen here
attempts—makes the rule of principle and hence the rule of law impossible. The
constitutional analogue of equality as a moral principle is, of course, equal
protection of the laws understood as the equal protection of equal rights. And
there can be little doubt that Lincoln's view was perfectly expressed in the
language of section one of the Fourteenth Amendment.

Westen, along with other leading commentators, would convert the Fourteenth Amendment's equal protection clause into an "instrument of revolution"[53] by interpreting the rights protected therein as rights that adhere to one's
class status rather than one's individual equality.[54] Westen, no less than Douglas
before him, seeks to minimize or extinguish the claims of equality for explicitly

racial purposes. This is made more than abundantly clear in his discussion of equal protection:

> It is emphatically true that the equal protection clause has legal and moral sub-stance, substance as significant and enduring as any norm of our society. The framers of the fourteenth amendment, having triumphed in war against slavery, enacted the equal protection clause to radically transform national notions of racial justice. It would be a mistake, however, to think that these notions of racial justice have anything in particular to do with the idea that likes should be treated alike. They are independent rights . . . *[R]ights of race and sex* can be stated without reference to 'likes,' or 'equals.' Indeed, not only can they be so stated, they must be so stated, because they provide the standards by which people are rendered 'alike' or 'unalike.'[55]

Westen thus reveals the ultimate motive for his attack on the idea of equality. Equality cannot comprehend the "rights of race and sex." These must be inde-pendent of any consideration of equality, because equality, rightly understood, denies that rights can adhere to one's class status. But once the idea of equality is severed from the notion of rights—once, that is, all notions of right are positive—there is no interest that cannot be disguised in terms of rights. What the proponents of class rights do not seem to realize is that once all right is deemed to be positive, there is no guarantee that class rights will remain in the service of the liberal state.

Indeed, the notion that rights adhere to class makes any principled applica-tion of equal protection impossible. Equal protection rights—flowing from the idea of natural human equality—have always been premised upon the proposi-tion that "[t]he rights created by the first section of the Fourteenth Amendment are, by its terms, guaranteed to the individual. The rights established are per-sonal rights."[56] This was certainly the view of a majority of those who debated the adoption of the Fourteenth Amendment in Congress. Senator Nye, for ex-ample, stated that

> We know the cause of our difficulties, and we may know, if we will, that there is but one remedy for the future. That remedy lies in equalized protection under equal laws. . . . Our fathers started with a new doctrine and a new theory. They threw aside the postulates of aristocracy, and started out on the plan of instituting govern-ment to protect natural and personal rights. . . . I am content to allow their simple idea of 'inalienable rights' to stand as my creed and the creed of the great Union party.[57]

This view was echoed at various times in the House by such luminaries as Bingham, Stevens, Wilson, Rogers, and Windom, among others, and in the Senate by Sumner, Lane, and others.

The insistence upon treating equal protection rights as class rights severs those rights from the necessary ground of equality. It inevitably promotes the notion—as Westen would have us believe—that all right is positive right, based exclusively on claims to power or privilege. The notion of positive right can provide no ground for the common good, the necessary precondition for the rule of law. The Framers believed that by nature individuals were the recipients of rights and that this was an irrefragable dictate of natural human equality. And as equality is our access to natural right, so it is our access to the common good and the rule of law. Abraham Lincoln called equality "the father of all moral principle."[58] The principle of equality, Lincoln argued, was in America the authoritative source of our most authoritative opinions. It was authoritative because it was grounded in the most authoritative of all sources—nature.

Today, it is hardly an exaggeration to say that "significant numbers of people with influence over the development of the law no longer find [it] . . . credible, or at least no longer believe that there are natural rights that our institutions can identify with enough precision to justify coercive resolution of disputes on the basis that natural rights require a particular resolution."[59] Contemporary commentators view the natural rights philosophy of the Framers as the "ghost" of the Constitution. As modern science has taught us the nonexistence of ghosts, so has it taught us the nonexistence of natural law or natural right. Thus, the Constitution must be severed from its ground in natural right. This is precisely what Stephen Douglas tried to do in formulating his "squatter sovereignty" doctrine, which would allow local majorities to determine the issue of slavery according to their interests. Lincoln objected that rights could never be rendered safe on the unstable foundation of interest. It can always be found in someone's interest to enslave another. Lincoln's opposition to Douglas was grounded in natural right principles—the only ground available to counter the argument that "justice is the interest of the stronger." Today we have obviously forgotten the lesson of Lincoln's victory over Douglas, as our most sophisticated legal commentators urge us to think of rights as merely assertions of power or privilege on the part of those who are powerful enough to make good on their claims. But such lapses of memory are dangerous, because we seem also to have forgotten the fragile character of political life itself.

NOTES

1 Alexander Hamilton, "The Farmer Refuted," in Harold C. Syrett et al., eds., *The Papers of Alexander Hamilton,* 26 vols. (New York: Columbia University Press, 1961–1978), 1:136.
2 James Wilson, "Considerations on the Nature and Extent of the Legislative Authority of the British Parliament," in Robert G. McCloskey, ed., *The Works of James Wilson,* 2 vols. (Cambridge: Harvard University Press, 1967), 2:727.
3 Theophilus Parsons, "The Essex Result," in Charles S. Hyneman and Donald S. Lutz, eds., *American Political Writing During the Founding Era, 1760–1805,* 2 vols. (Indianapolis: Liberty Press, 1983), 1:499–500.

4 Max Farrand, ed., *The Records of the Federal Convention of 1787,* 4 vols. (New Haven: Yale University Press, 1966), 2:476–477.

5 William Van der Weyde, ed., *The Life and Works of Thomas Paine,* 10 vols. (New Rochelle, NY: Thomas Paine National Historical Association, 1925), 6:232, 236.

6 Roy P. Basler, ed., *The Collected Works of Abraham Lincoln,* 9 vols. (New Brunswick, NJ: Rutgers University Press, 1953), 3:376.

7 *Life and Works of Thomas Paine,* 2:318–319.

8 *The Federalist* No. 39, Clinton Rossiter, ed. (New York: 1961), p. 240; No. 43, p. 279; see also No. 40, p. 253, No. 78, p. 469. Madison's argument was used by John Bingham in the debate over the Fourteenth Amendment in 1866. *Congressional Globe,* 39th Cong., 1st Sess., 1089 (1866): "And when the question was asked of one of the fathers of the Constitution, how can you break up the Confederation without the consent of all the States, and against the protest of some of them; how can you break the covenant of 'perpetual Union' under the Articles of Confederation? he gave for answer, that the right of the people to self-preservation justifies it; it rests upon the transcendent right of nature, and nature's God. That right is still in the people and has justified their action through all this trial."

9 *Trimble v. Gordon,* 430 U.S. 762, 777 (1976) (Rehnquist, J., dissenting).

10 See e.g., Bingham's remarks in *Congressional Globe,* 39th Cong., 1st Sess., 1034, and similar remarks at 1090, 1117 (1866).

11 *Collected Works of Abraham Lincoln,* 2:406.

12 *Congressional Globe,* 39th Cong., 1st Sess., 866 (1866).

13 Ibid. See also the remarks of Rep. Tobias A. Plants, at 1012.

14 Ibid.

15 Ibid., 2459.

16 See Robert Kaczorowski, "Searching for the Intent of the Framers of the Fourteenth Amendment," *Connecticut Law Review,* 5 (1973), pp. 368, 379, 382, 388, 392–393, 394 n. 67; H. Hyman and W. Wiecek, *Equal Justice Under Law* (New York: 1982), pp. 400–401, 403, 405, 492.

17 See, e.g., *Congressional Globe,* 39th Cong., 1st Sess., 726, 738, 869, 1077–1078, among many passages that could be cited.

18 Thomas Grey, "Do We Have an Unwritten Constitution?" *Stanford Law Review,* 27 (1975), p. 716.

19 Typical of the frequent references to natural rights in the Reconstruction debates are those of Senator Nye on February 28, 1866, *Congressional Globe,* 39th Cong., 1st Sess., 1069 (1866).

20 See Madison's essay "Universal Peace" published in the *National Gazette,* January 31, 1792, in Robert A. Rutland and Charles F. Hobson, eds., *The Papers of James Madison,* 16 vols. to date (Chicago: University of Chicago Press; Charlottesville: University Press of Virginia, 1962-   ), 14:206.

21 Harry Jaffa, *Crisis of the House Divided: An Interpretation of the Lincoln-Douglas Debates* (New York: Doubleday, 1959).

22 Leo Strauss, *Natural Right and History* (Chicago: University of Chicago Press, 1953), p. 3.

23 See Walter Murphy, "An Ordering of Constitutional Values," *Southern California Law Review,* 53 (1980), p. 712.

24 *Adamson v. Calif.*, 332 U.S. 46, 75 (1947) (Black, J., dissenting).

25 J. H. Ely, *Democracy and Distrust* (Cambridge: Harvard University Press, 1980), pp. 43–63. Surprisingly, Ely does not say who comprises the "reasoning class" or whether he counts himself as one of the class.

26 Michael Perry, *The Constitution, the Courts, and Human Rights* (New Haven: Yale University Press, 1982), p. 10 (emphasis added).

27 The language of "equal dignity and respect" can easily lead to some rather bizarre constitutional doctrines. See Ronald Dworkin, *Taking Rights Seriously* (Cambridge: Harvard University Press, 1978), pp. 198–199, 200–201, 226–227, suggests that anti-riot laws constitute a denial of "equal dignity and respect" (an "assault on human personality") because "a man cannot express himself freely when he cannot match his *rhetoric* to his outrage" (emphasis added). The Supreme Court has also begun to speak of the "personal right" "to be treated with equal dignity and respect."

28 *A Theory of Justice* (Cambridge: Harvard University Press, 1971), p. 47; this is, of course, an old position, albeit in a slightly new guise, but certainly advanced at a more propitious time than ever before. See Strauss, *Natural Right and History,* pp. 68–69.

29 Ibid., p. 15.

30 Ibid., 107.

31 See Strauss, *Natural Right and History,* p. 89–90.

32 *The Works of James Wilson,* 1:126–127.

33 Strauss, *Natural Right and History,* p. 141.

34 *Nicomachean Ethics,* 1134b 16ff.

35 Letter to Roger C. Weightman, June 24, 1826, in Merrill D. Peterson, ed., *Jefferson: Writings* (New York: Library of America, 1984), p. 1517.

36 "A Bill for Establishing Religious Freedom," in *Jefferson: Writings,* p. 346.

37 Ibid., p. 348.

38 Strauss, *Natural Right and History,* p. 148.

39 See Erler, "The Great Fence to Liberty: The Right to Property in the American Founding," in Ellen F. Paul and Howard Dickman, eds., *Liberty, Property, and the Foundations of the American Constitution* (Albany: State University of New York Press, 1989), pp. 43–63.

40 "Property" published in *The National Gazette,* March 27, 1792, in *The Papers of James Madison,* 14:266.

41 *The Federalist* No. 10, p. 78.

42 Ibid.

43 James Otis, *The Rights of the British Colonies Asserted and Proved* (Boston: 1764), 11–12 in Charles F. Mullett, ed., *Some Political Writings of James Otis,* University of Missouri Studies, Vol IV, no. 3 (July 1929), p. 310.

44 Letter to Roger Weightman, June 24, 1826, in *Jefferson: Writings,* p. 1517.

45 Letter to John Taylor, May 28, 1816, in ibid., p. 1392.

46 *Notes on the State of Virginia,* Query XVIII, in ibid., p. 289.

47 "The Farmer Refuted," *The Papers of Alexander Hamilton,* 1:87.

48 Michael Zuckert, "Justice Deserted: A Critique of Rawls' *A Theory of Justice,*" *Polity* 16 (Fall, 1981), pp. 476–477.

49 See Harvey Mansfield, Jr., *The Spirit of Liberalism* (Cambridge: Harvard University Press, 1978), pp. 72–74, 100–101.

50 Kenneth Karst, "Why Equality Matters," *Georgia Law Review* 17 (Winter, 1983), p. 249; See remarks of Senator Nye on Feb. 28, 1866: "It has often been said by unthinking men that the first clause in the Declaration of Independence was a mere rhetorical flourish without any practical meaning." *Congressional Globe,* 39th Cong., 1st Sess., 1077–1078.

51 Peter Westen, "The Empty Idea of Equality," *Harvard Law Review* 95 (January 1982), p. 565.

52 Ibid.

53 Henry S. Commager, "Equal Protection as an Instrument of Revolution," in Ronald Collins, ed., *Constitutional Government in America* (Durham, NC: Carolina Academic Press, 1980); See also, Justice William Brennan, "The Fourteenth Amendment," Address to the Section on Individual Rights and Responsibilities, American Bar Association, New York University Law School, August 8, 1986: the Fourteenth Amendment is "the amendment that served as the legal instrument of the egalitarian revolution that transformed contemporary American Society."

54 See Kenneth Karst and Harold Horowitz, "Affirmative Action and Equal Protection," *Virginia Law Review* 60 (October 1974), p. 955 with Chapter 5 of this volume.

55 Westen, p. 565 (emphasis added).

56 *Shelley v. Kraemer,* 334 U.S. 1, 22 (1948); *Missouri Ex Rel Gaines v. Canada,* 305 U.S. 337, 351 (1938).

57 *Congressional Globe,* 39th Cong., 1st Sess., 1074 (1866).

58 Speech at Chicago, IL, July 10, 1858 in *Collected Works of Abraham Lincoln,* 2:499.

59 Mark Tushnet, "The Relevance of the Framers' Natural Law Views to Contemporary Constitutional Interpretation," in Sarah B. Thurow, ed., *Constitutionalism in Perspective: The United States Constitution in Twentieth Century Politics* (Lanham, MD: University Press of America, 1988), p. 182.

Chapter Two

Majority Rule
and the Public Good

The task of the Framers of the Constitution was to set in motion the principles of the Declaration of Independence. Madison in the central number of the *Federalist* traces the ground of political right "to the transcendent law of nature and of nature's God, which declares that the safety and happiness of society are the objects at which all political institutions aim and to which all such institutions must be sacrificed" (No. 43, 279).[1] Only institutions derived from the laws of nature will thus be "honorable to human nature" (No. 36, 224; see No. 11, 91; No. 36, 217) in the sense of being grounded in the principles of human nature—those principles enunciated in the Declaration. As one prominent political philosopher has aptly stated, the Declaration

> expresses the conviction that there is a permanent order in the universe by which human beings ought, directly or indirectly, to be guided, whether as men or as citizens.
>
> This conviction—the heart of the Declaration—is also the one upon which the idea of natural right—the idea of political philosophy—stands or falls.[2]

Insofar as the Constitution is based on the natural right principles of the Declaration it must be regarded as "organic law," not a law of nature itself but partaking of the laws of nature insofar as it attempts to establish reason as the foundation of the rule of law.

The principal requirement deriving from the principles of human nature is consent of the governed—an irrefragable dictate of natural human equality. As Madison expressed it in the *Federalist*, the Framers of the Constitution were animated by "that honorable determination which animates every votary of freedom to rest all our political experiments on the capacity of mankind for self-government" (No. 39, 240). Consent is a necessary requirement not only for the establishment of legitimate government, but also for its operation.[3] It is for this reason that Madison insists that the Constitution must be "strictly republican" in its "general form and aspect" (No. 39, 240). For no other form of government "would be reconcilable with the genius of the people of America [or] with the fundamental principles of the Revolution" (No. 39, 240). The "principles of the Revolution," of course, are the principles of the Declaration, and it may be inferred from this that Madison believed that those principles required a form of government in which frequent elections are designed to provide for the periodic renewal of the consent of the governed. The Framers clearly recognized that "[r]epublican theory" dictates that "[t]he fabric of American empire ought to rest on the solid basis of THE CONSENT OF THE PEOPLE. The streams of national power ought to flow immediately from that pure, original fountain of all legitimate authority" (No. 22, 152; No. 49, 313–314).

It is true that in egalitarian natural right, consent takes precedence over wisdom. But the task of the statesmanship of the American Founding, as understood by Madison and the leading Framers, was to reconcile, insofar as possible, the requirements of consent and wisdom. After all, the goal of the Framers was not only to establish republican government, but just government as well. As Madison remarked in the fifty-first number of the *Federalist*, "[j]ustice is the end of government. It is the end of civil society. It ever has been and ever will be pursued until it be obtained, or until liberty be lost in the pursuit" (No. 51, 324). From this statement, it appears that liberty is the necessary, but not sufficient, condition of justice. Not only therefore must the people of America possess a "manly spirit [of] . . . freedom," (No. 57, 353) but they must also possess a well-defined "consciousness of unjust or dishonorable purposes" (No. 10, 83; No. 63, 385).

In the Constitutional Convention Pierce Butler remarked that "[w]e must follow the example of Solon who gave the Athenians not the best Gov[ernmen]t he could devise; but the best they w[ou]ld receive."[4] But Madison demonstrated a superior understanding of statesmanship in his answer to Butler:

We ought to consider what was right & necessary in itself for the attainment of a proper Governm[en]t. A plan adjusted to this idea will recommend itself—The respectability of this convention will give weight to their recommendation of it. Experience will be constantly urging the adoption of it and all the most enlightened & respectable citizens will be its advocates. Should we fall short of the necessary & proper point, this influential class of citizens will be turned against the plan, and little support in opposition to them can be gained to it from the unreflecting multitude.[5]

Madison, of course, was not unmindful of the importance of public opinion. In his 1791 essay, "Opinion," he wrote that "[p]ublic opinion sets bounds to every government, and is the real sovereign in every free one."[6] Thus even "the most rational government will not find it a superfluous advantage to have the prejudices of the community on its side" (No. 49, 315). But Madison certainly had a greater faith in the capacity of the people to choose on the basis of informed or enlightened opinion than did Butler or such "celebrated reformers" as Solon (No. 38, 233; No. 15, 107; No. 16, 117; No. 29, 187; No. 37, 227; No. 60, 367; No. 77, 464). For as Madison noted in 1792, it is the leading characteristic of a representative republic that it "*chuses* the wisdom, of which hereditary aristocracy has the *chance.*"[7] But, of course, it requires an active and enlightened citizenry, although not possessing wisdom itself, to choose wisdom.

Indeed, the Framers self-consciously looked upon the experiment of the American Founding as an attempt "to decide the important question, whether societies of men are really capable or not of establishing good government from reflection and choice, or whether they are forever destined to depend for their political constitutions on accident and force" (No. 1, 33). The failure of the experiment would not only be a disaster for America, but would "deserve to be considered as the general misfortune of mankind" (No. 1, 33; No. 36, 224). Political and social conditions in America were so propitious for the success of the experiment that a failure there would most likely mean the end of all attempts to establish republican government anywhere in the world. America was almost a clean slate, with no ancien regime to destroy. Except for slavery (an enormous exception), Americans were already enjoying equality and almost everyone who desired to do so had the prospect of land ownership. The American experiment would therefore, in all probability, "decide forever the fate of Republican Government."[8] It was therefore the principal task of the authors of the *Federalist* to "promote the cause of truth and lead to a right judgment of the true interests of the community."[9]

What are "the true interests of the community?" The primitive purpose of civil society is, of course, safety—the first object of a "wise and free people" (No. 3, 42). But the necessary conditions of civil society are not its sufficient conditions. Accordingly, the *Federalist* is more apt to speak of the "safety and welfare," the "safety and happiness," or sometimes just the "public happiness' of the people. More often, however, the *Federalist* describes the ends of civil society in terms of "the public good," "justice and the public good," or "the permanent and aggregate interests of the community" (No. 10, 80, 78). Or as Madison elaborated this theme in the forty-fifth number, "the public good, the real welfare of the great body of the people, is the supreme object to be pursued; and that no form of government whatever has any other value than as it may be fitted for the attainment of this object" (No. 45, 289). In the actual apportionment of power to secure the public good, it is simply a matter of discriminating the "necessary means of attaining a necessary end."

> [I]n all cases where power is to be conferred, the point first to be decided is whether such a power be necessary to the public good; as the next will be, in case of an affirmative decision, to guard as effectually as possible against a perversion of the power to the public detriment (No. 41, 255–256).

In popular forms of government, however, the public good always has a questionable status.[10] The reason is simple: "violent factions [are] the natural offspring of free government" (No. 43, 273). Indeed, such factions "have, in truth, been the mortal diseases under which popular governments have everywhere perished" (No. 10, 77). Madison defined faction as "a number of citizens whether amounting to a majority or minority of the whole who are united and actuated by some common impulse of passion, or of interest, adverse to the rights of other citizens, or to the permanent and aggregate interests of the community" (No. 10, 78). The "permanent and aggregate interests" seem to refer to a distinction that Madison introduces a few paragraphs later: the public good and private rights. The "aggregate interests" comprise the protection of the private rights of the various interests that compose society; the "permanent" interests would therefore correspond to the public good. The public good is more than the sum of the "aggregate interests" of society. Some interests are "adverse" both to the public good and private rights; but not all are. The distinction is whether they are consistent with the public good—that is, both the "permanent and aggregate interests of the community."

Minority faction is not a major concern because "the republican principle . . . enables the majority to defeat its sinister views by regular vote" (No. 10, 80). A minority faction "may clog the administration, it may convulse the society; but it will be unable to execute and mask its violence under the forms of the Constitution" (No. 10, 80). But, as Madison continues, "[w]hen a majority is included in a faction, the form of popular government, on the other hand, enables it to sacrifice to its ruling passion or interest both the public good and the rights of other citizens" (No. 10, 80). The goal of the *Federalist's* constitutional statesmanship therefore is to find a republican solution to the problem of majority faction: "To secure the public good and private rights against the danger of such a faction, and at the same time to preserve the spirit and form of popular government, is then the great object to which our inquiries are directed" (No. 10, 80). For only a constitutional scheme that provides a "republican remedy for the diseases most incident to republican government" can rescue republican government "from the opprobrium under which it has so long labored" (No. 10, 84, 81).

The public good and private rights are indeed the appropriate objects of republican statesmanship. In free government the requirements of the public good are often in tension with the protection of private rights. Since a large part of the public purpose of republican government is the protection of private rights, republics will find it especially difficult to provide support for the public good. Citizens in republics such as the one contemplated by the Framers are more likely to indulge an introspective concern for their private rights (and privacy generally) than to devote themselves to the public good. A concern for privacy is natural in free government; the public good will be the product of the statesman's art. And although there is no necessary or inevitable contradiction between these two essential ingredients of republicanism, reconciling the public good and private rights provides the largest challenge to republican statesmanship. One not entirely trivial example is the case of the Constitution's protection of copyrights and patents where, Madison notes, "[t]he public good fully coincides in both cases with the claims of individuals" (No. 43, 272). But, of course, the Framers had to come to grips with the much larger issues of majority faction—that rock upon which all previous attempt to establish republican government had foundered.

Every form of government involves a ruling and a ruled element. The ruling element—whether oligarchic, aristocratic or democratic—is necessarily only a part of the whole. As Madison remarked in his "Vices of the Political System," a document that he composed in preparation for the Constitutional Convention, it is "the fundamental principle of republican Government that the majority who rule in such Governments are the safest Guardians both of the public good and of private rights."[11] But this fundamental principle of republicanism was not self-executing. In a letter written to Thomas Jefferson shortly after the close of the Convention, Madison noted that "a prudent regard to private or partial good, as essentially involved in the general and permanent good of the whole" should "be sufficient of itself" to render the majority a safe representative of the public interest. But as Madison continued: "Experience however shews that it has little effect on individuals, and perhaps still less on a collection of individuals, and least of all on a majority with the public authority in their hands. If the former are ready to forget that honesty is the best policy, the last do more. They often proceed on the converse of the maxim: that whatever is politic is honest."[12] While a "consciousness of unjust or dishonorable purposes" and the prudent policy of "self-interest rightly understood" will be important constraints upon the majority, the "fundamental principle of republican government" requires for its efficacy a well-constructed constitution designed to obviate the problem of majority faction by more direct and powerful means. The object of republican statesmanship as understood by the Framers was to contrive a constitutional structure whereby the part could rule in the interest of the whole. In terms that Madison used in later years, some constitutional contrivance was necessary to translate a "numerical majority of the people" into "a political and constitutional majority."[13] Constitutional majorities would be capable of ruling in the interest of the whole and would therefore be a safe (or at least comparatively safe) repository of the public good. They would, in short, be just majorities.

Madison noted that there are two methods of removing the causes of faction—both incompatible with republican government. The first was to destroy the liberty "which is essential to its existence." Faction could indeed be prevented by the destruction of liberty, but since liberty is "essential to political life" this would be a "remedy . . . worse than the disease" (No. 10, 78). Liberty is essential to "political life" and not just to popular regimes. The reason is that rulers in every form of government need liberty to rule. In popular government the ruling or sovereign element is the people and liberty therefore is an essential means to justice in popular forms of government, but most particularly republican government. The second method of removing the causes of faction adumbrated by Madison is to give "to every citizen the same opinions, the same passions, and the same interests" (No. 10, 78). Whereas the first method is "unwise," the second is deemed by Madison to be "impracticable." The reason is human nature: "the latent causes of faction . . . are sown in the nature of man" (No. 10, 79). Any attempt therefore to create a uniformity of passion, opinion, and interests—a situation in which the common good would no longer be problematic[14]—is thus bound to fail because it would do violence to human nature. The degradation of human nature that would be required for such a project could be the product only of the most tyrannical regimes. "Theoretic politicians," Madison wrote, "have erroneously supposed that by reducing mankind to a perfect equality in their political rights, they would at the same time be perfectly equalized and assimilated in their possessions, their opinions, and their passions" (No. 10, 81).

As Harry Jaffa accurately comments, the Anti-Federalist "advocates of small republics, whom Madison characterizes as 'theoretic politicians' . . . seem to have been doctrinaires of a kind of utopian agrarianism, in which faction was overcome by something akin to Rousseau's general will (by which, we recall, men might be 'forced to be free')."[15] Human nature does not render the assimilation of opinions, passions, and interests impossible, but only impracticable. It is impracticable in a free society that seeks its authoritative ground in the transcendent laws of nature and nature's God. For only such a society can honor human nature. A regime rooted in the principles of natural right will be moderated by a commonsensical appreciation of the limits of human nature. Marxism, for example, does not recognize the existence of human nature and regimes based on Marxist ideology therefore must degrade human nature by terror and violence to make it conform to the goals promised in the name of the historical-material-dialectic—goals that promise nothing less than the complete relief of the human estate.[16]

Powerful attributes of human nature militate against the practicability of assimilating opinions, passions, and interests. The first is the fallibility of human reason: "As long as the reason of man continues fallible, and he at liberty to exercise it, different opinions will be formed" (No. 10, 78). Human reason is defective because of the connection that subsists between reason and self-love. This will insure that opinions and passions "will have a reciprocal influence on each other; and the former will be objects to which the latter will attach themselves (No. 10, 78). If human reason were infallible—that is, if reason could be exercised apart from the influence of passion or self-love—the common good would not be problematic. This would be the enviable situation of a community of gods or a "nation of philosophers" (No. 49, 315), although, curiously enough, Madison writes that "[h]ad every Athenian citizen been a Socrates, every Athenian assembly would have been a mob" (No. 55, 342).

An "insuperable obstacle to a uniformity of interests" rests in "[t]he diversity in the faculties of men, from which the rights of property originate" (No. 10, 78). And, Madison continues,

[t]he protection of these faculties is the first object of government. From the protection of different and unequal faculties of acquiring property, the possession of different degrees and kinds of property immediately results; and from the influence of these on the sentiments and views of the respective proprietors ensues a division of the society into different interests and parties (No. 10, 78).

If human beings did not possess "different and unequal faculties" there would not be "different degrees and kinds of property." Under these circumstances, the natural form of human community would be communism. But the protection of property is not only a recognition of natural human diversity, but the protection of its manifold expression in different degrees and kinds of property as well as a legitimation of "different interests and parties" in society.[17] One commentator has noticed that whereas Locke posits the protection of property as the purpose of civil society, Madison's formulation is more extensive since he says that the protection of the "faculties of acquiring property" is the "first object of government." This, of course, is the protection of the potential for acquisition rather than the protection of any particular acquisition, and the implication seems to be that not all faculties result in the acquisition of property in Locke's sense.[18] Whereas the different faculties for acquisition exist by nature, civil society is necessary to secure their exercise. Thus it may be true that the protection of the different faculties is necessary for public happiness, which in turn is an indispensable part of the public good.

Madison concludes that the latent potential for faction is "sown in the nature of man" and will actualize itself in a variety of ways "according to the circumstances of civil society" (No. 10, 79). Thus faction seems not only to be "sown in the nature of man," but also in need of civil society to protect the "liberty" without which it would not exist. Thus Madison seems to imply that man is naturally political, and will naturally form political opinions to which he will passionately attach himself, i.e., will naturally participate in politics. And it seems that there is almost no human endeavor that will not serve as the occasion for factious combinations, and where no "substantial occasion presents itself the most frivolous and fanciful distinctions have been sufficient to kindle their unfriendly passions and excite their most violent conflicts (No. 10, 79; No. 34, 208).

There is one source of faction, however, that has a constant operation on society: "the most common and durable source of factions has been the various and unequal distribution of property. Those who hold and those who are without property have ever formed distinct interests in society" (No. 10, 79). Under these circumstances majority faction will be inevitable as the many who are without property will form factious combinations against those few who are the holders of property and wealth. But the destruction of the property rights of the few is no less an unjust act than the disfranchisement of the poor.

The pressing problem in 1787 was not the conflict between rich and poor, but between debtors and creditors. Debtors, the majority of whom were farmers, demanded the issuance of paper currency and the suspension of payments of debt. As it has often been noted, Shay's rebellion served to underscore both the urgency and importance of both the Annapolis and Philadelphia conventions. Thoughtful men knew that a direct assault on property in the form of legal suspensions of contractual obligations would merely be a prelude to the dissolution of civil society. As Jaffa cogently notes,

> The problem of faction [in 1787] was very largely one of preventing the interest of farmers from unjustly dominating those of the others. The problem would have been insoluble, if the agricultural interest was homogeneous, if, that is, farmers were not divided by local attachments, as well as between those who raised grain and those who—for example—raised cotton, tobacco, rice, or pork. Any ideological consolidation of the agricultural interest could enable it to ride roughshod over the other competing interests. Nothing bespeaks Hamilton's and Madison's constitutional purposes—or their reasons for writing the *Federalist*—more than the prohibitions laid upon the states in the Constitution, to coin money, to emit bills of credit, to impair the obligation of contracts.[19]

The protection of property takes on an especial importance because it is the most visible expression of the rights of human nature. Indeed, it was the Framers' view that republican government could not exist without strong protection for property rights. The false dichotomy that is often drawn today between property rights and human rights would have struck the Framers as certainly bizarre, even though they were surely aware of Rousseau's critique of the private right of property in the *Second Discourse*—known best today in its various Marxist guises. Madison understood that the right to property was, at bottom, the comprehensive right: "as a man is said to have a right to his property, he may be equally said to have a property in his rights."[20] Threats against liberty will be felt first as threats against property rights—in the form of unjust taxes, the impairment of the obligations of contracts, or other disfranchisements of property rights. If the people wait until their liberties are threatened directly then it is likely that the forces of oppression are already too strong to be resisted. Property is the most visible form of human freedom (since it results from the diversity of human nature) and as such serves as an early warning of threats upon liberty. The time to be alarmed for liberty is at the first sign of trespass against property rights, since a trespass against property is at one and the same time a trespass against life and liberty, property having the same natural right status as both life and liberty.

In addition to the factions that result from the unequal distribution of property, there are those that are produced by the "various distribution" (No. 10, 79). There are creditors and debtors, a landed interest, a mercantile interest, a moneyed interest, and "many lesser interests [that] grow up of necessity in civilized nations, and divide them into different classes, actuated by different sentiments and views" (No. 10, 79). The civilized nations that produce such a multiplicity of interests would today be called capitalist nations—those with free market economies. Various interests result from the policy of making the protection of the "diverse faculties of acquiring property" the "first object of government." This "various" distribution of property cuts across the distinction between rich and poor, dividing the nation into interests rather than classes. A rich debtor and a rich creditor will always disagree about political issues involving inflation, the former favoring policies that encourage inflation, the latter policies that discourage the devaluation of the money owed him. Both may agree, however, on other political issues. Similarly the workers in the various branches of manufacturing might have the same interest as those who own the manufacturing plant in matters involving import quotas; and differ with workers in agricultural or mercantile sectors because they have competing economic interests. It is not their class—either in the case of the rich or the poor— that determines their opinions, but their interests. As Martin Diamond noted, "in the extended republic the conflict of limited and specific interests replaces the divisive and general struggle between two great classes. In this sense, Madison anticipated and refuted Marxism. Rather than compacting into two distinct great classes, in Madison's theory, rich and poor are fragmented and jumbled together into narrow and particular 'factions'."[21]

Madison notes that "[t]he regulation of the various and interfering interests forms the principal task of modern legislation and involves the spirit of party and faction in the necessary and ordinary operations of government" (No. 10,

79). The "first object of government," however, was earlier said to be the protection of the diverse faculties "from which the rights of property originate." Legislation, of course, is not as comprehensive as the "first object of government." They are related to one another as means to end. Therefore, the object of the regulation will be to insure that there will be vigorous competition between the various interests. But this will necessarily involve the "spirit of party and faction," since in republican government there seems to be no vantage point or will independent of society that can look beyond the interests of the various parties. "What are the different classes of legislators," Madison asks, "but advocates and parties to the causes which they determine?" (No. 10, 79). No doubt "[j]ustice ought to hold the balance between them. Yet the parties are, and must be, themselves the judges; and the most numerous party, or in other words, the most powerful faction must be expected to prevail" (No. 10, 80). Thus decisions will not be made "with a sole regard to justice and the public good" (No. 10, 80). Indeed, it would require "enlightened statesmen" to render these clashing interests "subservient to the public good." But, as Madison laconically notes, "[e]nlightened statesmen will not always be at the helm" (No. 10, 80).

Enlightened statesmen will sometimes be at the helm, however. The work of the Framers, among other things, testifies to this. An enlightened statesmen attempts to replace the partial views of the various parties with the comprehensive view of the public good. The enlightened statesman, although understanding the partial claims of the parties, remains detached from them, outside the clash of party interests. But enlightened statesmen are rare and are more likely to be called forth by great political crises than by the ordinary routine of governing. Thus it is safer for constitutional governments not to place too much reliance on the presence of those who can look beyond the parties to "indirect and remote considerations, which will rarely prevail over the immediate interest which one party may find in disregarding the rights of another or the good of the whole" (No. 10, 80). Any attempt to extinguish the clashing interests that naturally occur in civilized societies in the name of a common good that does not rest on the consent of the governed would render republicanism impossible. Thus, Madison concludes, since "the *causes* of faction cannot be removed" the "relief is only to be sought in the means of controlling its *effects*" (No. 10, 80).

There are two means by which the effects of faction can be controlled: "Either the existence of the same passion or interest in a majority at the same time must be prevented, or the majority, having such coexistent passion or interest, must be rendered, by their number and local situation, unable to concert and carry into effect schemes of oppression" (No. 10, 81). Given the coincidence of "the impulse and the opportunity," Madison notes, "neither moral nor religious motives can be relied on as an adequate control" (No. 10, 81). Moral and religious motives are inadequate to control "the injustice and violence of individuals" and "lose their efficacy" even more in larger numbers and particularly in political bodies. Morality and religion are obviously not complete bars to injustice and violence either of individuals or factions, but they serve as the necessary basis for the "consciousness of unjust and dishonorable purposes" that serves as a necessary—but not sufficient—limit on majority faction.

But the extended sphere and consequent multiplicity of interests will be more efficacious than moral and religious motives:

> Extend the sphere and you take in a greater variety of parties and interests; you make it less probable that a majority of the whole will have a common motive to invade the rights of other citizens; or if such a common motive exists, it will be more difficult for all who feel it to discover their own strength and to act in unison with each other. Besides other impediments, it may be remarked that, where there is a consciousness of unjust or dishonorable purposes, communication is always checked by distrust in proportion to the number whose concurrence is necessary (No. 10, 83).

In a large, diverse republic, Madison reasoned, it will rarely be in the *interest* of the majority to invade the rights of the minority. Since, in all probability, there will be no permanent class interests in society, it is unlikely that there will be permanent majorities and permanent minorities; thus, the majority will never develop a sense of its own identity and interest *as a majority*. In such a situation, there is greater likelihood that these majorities will be "political and constitutional," i.e., just majorities capable of ruling in the interest of the whole because there will be no "common motive" to invade the rights of the minority or of individuals. As Madison noted in the fifty-first number, "[d]ifferent interests necessarily exist in different classes of citizens. If a majority be united by a common interest, the rights of the minority will be insecure." The republican method "of providing against this evil" is "by comprehending in the society so many separate descriptions of citizens as will render an unjust combination of a majority of the whole very improbable, if not impracticable" (No. 51, 323–324).

The majorities that do form will be essentially composed of coalitions of minorities that come together for limited, self-interested purposes; as private interest groups they remain largely unaffected by the fact that they have become a part of the majority. Under these circumstances, only moderate or middle ground political positions can hope to garner majority support. When political positions become extreme, the foundation of the majority coalition—the necessary ground for consensus—itself will be compromised. Different majorities will be formed as the political issues themselves change. In this manner the various minorities that compose the majority never develop a sense of being a permanent part of the majority and therefore are not able to calculate their own interests accordingly. The best security is to prevent the majority from ever having an interest in invading the rights of the minority. In an extensive republic containing a "great variety of interest, parties and sects . . . a coalition of a majority of the whole society could seldom take place on any other principles than those of justice and the general good." Since there will be "less danger to a minor from the will of the major party, there must be less pretext also, to provide for the security of the former, by introducing into the government a will not dependent on the latter; or in other words, a will independent of the society itself" (No. 51, 325). It is important to note, however, that Madison indicates that a majority faction will "seldom" form. As long as society is governed by the will of the majority, majority faction is always possible. There is no method of absolutely preventing majority faction without introducing "a will independent of society itself," a remedy that is incompatible with republican government itself. Based on the principles of republican government, the best that can be done is to render majority faction unlikely.

The competition between the various interests in the extended commercial republic provides the necessary conditions for "subjecting the will of society to the reason of the society." It produces a kind of "equipoise of [the] passions [in which] reason [is] free to decide for the public good."[22] Thus it is clear that the public good is not simply the by-product of the various and competing interests in society. Rather, the public good will find its ground in the reason of the public. The reason of the public is necessarily the foundation of republicanism because republican government is derived from universal principles. Constitutionalism and the rule of law rest on reason, not will. As Madison remarked in the forty-ninth number, "it is the reason, alone, of the public, that ought to control and regulate the government. The passions ought to be controlled and regulated by the government" (No. 49, 317). But as Madison also noted, "the mild voice of reason, pleading the cause of an enlarged and permanent interest, is but too often drowned, before public bodies as well as individuals, by the clamors of an impatient avidity for immediate and immoderate gain" (No. 42, 268). In a similar vein, Hamilton wrote that

> [t]he republican principle demands that the deliberate sense of the community should govern the conduct of those to whom they intrust the management of their affairs; but it does not require an unqualified complaisance to every sudden breeze of passion, or to every transient impulse which the people may receive from the arts of man, who flatter their prejudices to betray their interests. It is a just observation that the people commonly *intend* the PUBLIC GOOD. This often applies to their very errors. But their good sense would despise the adulator who should pretend that they always *reason right* about the *means* of promoting it (No. 71, 432).

If "enlightened statesmen will not always be at the helm," what will be the source of the public's reason?

It must be recalled that Madison had defined faction as springing "from some common impulse of passion, or of interest, adverse to the rights of other citizens, or to the permanent and aggregate interests of the community." Madison does not include here "a number of citizens" united and actuated by common opinion. It is true that shortly after the definition of faction Madison asserts the "reciprocal influence" of passion and opinion, but he does not intimate that passion will furnish the objects of opinion, but, on the contrary that opinions will be the objects of the passions. Thus as one recent commentator has expressed it, Madison "maintains a certain independence and even dignity for opinion: men are divided in their opinions not so much on account of the influence of passion but due to the fallibility of reason." There is no doubt that part of the "fallibility of human reason may well be the obscurantism of the passions; but [Madison] emphasizes that fallible men typically make mistakes in their reasoning . . . not that they are biased or unjust." This same commentator concludes that "[t]he refusal to reduce opinions or reason to the effect of prerational or subrational causes is characteristic of *Federalist* 10's argument, and lays the groundwork for the politics of public opinion—of republicanism—that *The Federalist* is constructing."[23] It is precisely this independence for opinion that lays the basis for the reason of the public—or "the politics of public opinion." Passions, although subordinate to reason, cannot be ruled by reasoned argument or persuasion. Because opinion can exist independently of the passions, it can be informed by reasoned argument. And it is in the sphere of opinion that the reason of the public will emerge in republican government.

It should be noted here that Madison's examination of opinion in *Federalist* 10 and throughout the *Federalist* differs from that of Hobbes. Hobbes had sought to subordinate reason to passion in order to minimize differences among men with respect to the ends of government. In his famous statement in the *Leviathan,* Hobbes had remarked that "the Thoughts, are to the Desires, as Scouts and Spies, to range abroad, and find the way to the things Desired: All Stedinesse of the minds motion, and all quicknesse of the same, proceeding from thence."[24] But for Madison and the Framers generally the whole thrust of constitutional government was to insure that the reason of the public ultimately ruled its passions. Reason is therefore not instrumental to the passions, but the source of the public good that excludes those "impulses of passion or interest." In rejecting Hobbes on the possibility of a public happiness based on the reason of the public, Madison seems to be pointing to an older tradition originated by Aristotle.[25]

The *Federalist,* of course, does not expect to create a "nation of philosophers" where "a reverence for the laws would be sufficiently inculcated by the voice of an enlightened reason" (No. 49, 315). The authors of the *Federalist* were well aware that government is necessary "[b]ecause the passions of men will not conform to the dictates of reason and justice without constraint" (No. 15, 110; No. 51, 322). But the greatest constraint in popular government is public opinion. As Madison noted in the forty-ninth number, "If it be true that all governments rest on opinion, it is no less true that the strength of opinion in

each individual, and its practical influence on his conduct, depend much on the
number which he supposes to have entertained the same opinion. The reason of
man, like man himself, is timid and cautious when left alone, and acquires
firmness and confidence in proportion to the number with which it is associated" (No. 49, 314–315). In 1791 when Madison wrote that "[p]ublic opinion sets bounds to every government, and is the real sovereign in every free
one" he also adumbrated the role of government in the formation of public
opinion. "As there are cases where the public opinion must be obeyed by the
government; so there are cases, where not being fixed, it may be influenced by
the government. This distinction, if kept in view, would prevent or decide
many debates on the respect due from the government to the sentiments of the
people. In proportion as government is influenced by opinion, it must be so, by
whatever influences opinion."[26]

Near the beginning of *Federalist* 10, Madison wrote that

> [c]omplaints are everywhere heard from our most considerate and virtuous citizens,
> equally the friends of public and private faith and of public and personal liberty,
> that our governments are too unstable, that the public good is disregarded in the
> conflicts of rival parties, and that measures are too often decided, not according to
> the rules of justice and the right of the minor party, but by the superior force of an
> interested and overbearing majority.

Presumably the "most considerate and virtuous citizens" can form their political opinions and interests out of a regard for the public good. Although their
number may be relatively small, they are the most suited to represent the public
reason. The difference between a republic and a pure democracy is, of course,
that the former operates by the principle of representation, which posits "the
total exclusion of the people in their collective capacity" from governing in
favor of representatives of the people (No. 63, 387). It is here that the people in
the ordinary act of self-government "choose wisdom." As Madison argues,
representation can

> refine and enlarge the public views by passing them through the medium of a
> chosen body of citizens, whose wisdom may best discern the true interests of their
> country and whose patriotism and love of justice will be least likely to sacrifice it to
> temporary or partial considerations. Under such a regulation it may well happen
> that the public voice, pronounced by the representatives of the people, will be more
> consonant to the public good than if pronounced by the people themselves, con-
> vened for the purpose (No. 10, 82).

But, of course, there is no guarantee that the people will indeed choose the wise
or the public spirited.

> On the other hand, the effect may be inverted. Men of factious tempers, of local
> prejudices, or of sinister designs, may, by intrigue, by corruption, or by other means,
> first obtain the suffrages, and then betray the interests of the people (No. 10, 82).

Representation is not merely a "mechanical power in government" (No. 14, 100) that allows for an extensive republic, but it is not sufficient in itself. If representation were sufficient, then the separation of powers would be superfluous. Not only must the separation of powers serve as "auxiliary precautions," but public opinion must be fortified as well.

A majority of the whole inspired by the same reasoned political opinion would not be a majority faction in terms of Madison's definition of faction as proceeding from some "impulse of passion or interest" adverse to "the permanent and aggregate interests of the community." Such a majority would, in fact, be the legitimate representative of the public good. A large part of the *Federalist's* project is to inform public opinion and, in effect, create partisans of republican principles. In *Federalist* No. 10, Madison notes that among the numerous "frivolous" sources of faction is a "zeal for different opinions concerning religion, concerning government, and many other points, as well of speculation as of practice." It is this "zeal" that has inclined men to be "much more disposed to vex and oppress each other than to cooperate for their common good" (No. 10, 79). In the peroration of the tenth number, however, Madison issues an invitation to partisanship: "In the extent and proper structure of the Union, therefore, we behold a republican remedy for the diseases most incident to republican government. And according to the degree of pleasure and pride we feel in being republicans ought to be our zeal in cherishing the spirit and supporting the character of federalists" (No. 10, 84). Republican pride thus finds its partisanship in federalism. This zeal is not a factious zeal because it is animated by a concern for the common good of the whole, not that of a part. The opponents of the Constitution, in contrast, are said to exhibit an "indiscrete zeal" (No. 44, 286). It may be only a short step from the partisan zeal that Madison invokes in support of the Constitution to a political party devoted to the partisanship of republican principles.[27] After all, Madison described the Republican party he helped found as "the best keeper of the people's liberties."[28]

Even though the political situation of the extended republic holds the prospect of creating an "equipoise of the passions," republican government presupposes a higher degree of virtue in the people than any other form of government. It is only too obvious that a self-governing people cannot be ruled by the "tyranny of [its] own passions" (No. 63, 384). And whereas "there is a degree of depravity in mankind which requires a certain degree of circumspection and distrust," republicanism places its "esteem and confidence" in those self-governing qualities of "human nature" that befit a free people. If there is not "sufficient virtue among men for self-government," Madison chided, then "nothing less than the chains of despotism can restrain them from destroying and devouring one another" (No. 55, 346).

Yet, the *Federalist* is a sober political work; it does not place unwarranted trust in an "exalted opinion of human virtue" (No. 75, 451)—what thoughtful political writer ever has? There is no doubt, however, that the policies of repub-lican government should "inspire a general prudence and industry" as well as "industry and morals" among the people" (No. 44, 283, 281). The *Federalist* does not, of course, undertake a thematic discussion of the question of virtue or morals. That would have been altogether inappropriate since these matters were never in dispute in the ratification debate. It probably would have been alto-gether imprudent to have broached such a subject as well. Rather, the question of virtue seems to have been subsumed under the recognized "genius of the people" and the "vigilant and manly spirit which actuates people of America—a spirit which nourishes freedom, and in return is nourished by it" (No. 57, 353). An extended republic embracing a multiplicity of interests with a consti-tutional structure integrated around the separation of powers will be the best guarantee of the "rational liberty" that is the product of "the cool and deliber-ate sense of the community" and is the hallmark "in all free governments" (No. 53, 331, No. 63, 384). "The aim of every political constitution," Madison writes in the fifty-seventh number, "is, or ought to be, first to obtain for rulers men who possess most wisdom to discern, and most virtue to pursue, the com-mon good of the society; and in the next place, to take the most effectual precautions for keeping them virtuous whilst they continue to hold their public trust." Elections are the "characteristic policy of republican government" for obtaining such men, but the "means relied on in this form of government for preventing their degeneracy are numerous and various" (No. 57, 350–351). The "numerous and various" means that Madison refers to here are contained within the complex dynamics of the separation of powers, dynamics that can supply "by opposite and rival interests, the defect of better motives" and give to the imprudent "inventions of prudence" (No. 51, 322).

NOTES

1   Throughout this chapter, references to the *Federalist* are indicated by paper and page number in the Clinton Rossiter edition of the *Federalist* (New York: Mentor, 1961).

2   Harry V. Jaffa, *How to Think About the American Revolution* (Durham, NC: Caro-lina Academic Press, 1978), pp. x–xi.

3   Ibid., pp. 75ff.

4   Max Farrand, ed., *The Records of the Federal Convention of 1787,* 4 vols. (New Haven: Yale University Press, 1966), 1:125; the same remark was made by Gun-ning Bedford, 1:491.

5   Ibid., 1:215, 528–529; see 1:366, 474 (Hamilton); 1:372 (Randolph).

6   "Public Opinion," *National Gazette,* 19 December 1791, Robert A. Rutland and Charles F. Hobson, eds., *The Papers of James Madison,* 16 vols. to date (Chicago: University of Chicago Press; Charlottesville: University Press of Virginia, 1962–), 14:170.

7   Ibid. 14:179.

8 Farrand, 1:423; see 1:452; 1:529.

9 "Preface" to the first edition, in Paul Leicester Ford, ed., *The Federalist Papers* (New York: Henry Holt, 1898), p. xxvii. Unfortunately the preface to the first edition has been omitted from all modern editions of *The Federalist*.

10 See Erler, "The Problem of the Public Good in *The Federalist*" *Polity*, 13 (1981, pp. 649–667). This earlier account, I now believe, undervalued the essential connection between the Declaration of Independence and the Constitution. In this earlier interpretation I had underestimated, not indeed the truth of the *Federalist's* argument, but its political import. See infra, Chapter 4, n. 13.

11 *Papers of James Madison*, 9:354.

12 Madison to Thomas Jefferson, Oct. 24, 1787, ibid., 10:213.

13 "Majority Governments," in Gaillard Hunt, ed., *The Writings of James Madison*, 9 vols. (New York: G. P. Putnam's Sons, 1900–1910), 9:527. This unpublished essay was probably written in 1833.

14 Madison to Thomas Jefferson, Oct. 24, 1787, *Papers of James Madison*, 10:212: "Theoretic writers . . . found their reasoning on the idea, that the people composing the Society, enjoy not only an equality of political rights; but that they have all precisely the same interests, and the same feelings in every respect. Were this in reality the case, their reasoning would be conclusive. The interest of the majority would be that of the minority also; the decisions could only turn on mere opinion concerning the good of the whole, of which the major voice would be the safest criterion."

15 *How to Think About the American Revolution*, p. 5.

16 See Edward Erler, "Solzhenitsyn" in Harry V. Jaffa, ed., *Essays in Statesmanship* (Durham, NC: Carolina Academic Press, 1981), p. 241.

17 See Edward Erler, "The Great Fence to Liberty: The Right to Property in the American Founding," in Ellen Frankel Paul and Howard Dickman, eds., *Liberty, Property, and the Foundations of the American Constitution* (Albany: State University of New York Press, 1989), pp. 43–63.

18 David F. Epstein, *The Political Theory of The Federalist* (Chicago: University of Chicago Press, 1984), p. 74.

19 Harry V. Jaffa, *American Conservatism and the American Founding* (Durham, NC: Carolina Academic Press, 1984), p. 207.

20 "Property," published in the *National Gazette*, 29 March 1792, in *The Papers of James Madison* 14:266. In 1829 in a speech to the Virginia Constitutional Convention," Madison said that "[i]t is sufficiently obvious, that persons and property are the two great subjects on which Governments are to act; and that the rights of persons, and their rights of property, are the objects, for the protection of which Government was instituted. These rights cannot well be separated. The personal right to acquire property, which is a natural right, gives to property, when acquired, a right to protection as a social right." *The Writings of James Madison*, 9:360–361.

21 Martin Diamond, *The Founding of the Democratic Republic* (Itasca, IL: F. E. Peacock Publishers, 1981), p. 73.

22 "Universal Peace," published in the *National Gazette*, 31 January 1792, in *The Papers of James Madison* 14:208.

23 Charles R. Kesler, "*Federalist* 10 and American Republicanism," in Charles R.

Kesler, ed., *Saving the Revolution: The Federalist Papers and the American Founding* (New York: The Free Press, 1987), pp. 26–27.

24 Thomas Hobbes, *Leviathan,* C.B. Macpherson, ed. (New York: Penguin Books, 1968), ch. viii, p. 139.

25 See Chapter 1, p. 17 and Epstein, *The Political Theory of The Federalist,* pp. 79, 124.

26 "Public Opinion," published in the *National Gazette,* 19 December 1791, in *The Papers of James Madison* 14:170.

27 See Sanderson Schaub, "Justice and Honor, the Surest Foundation of Liberty: The Natural Law Doctrine in *The Federalist* No. 10," in Sarah B. Thurow, ed., *To Secure the Blessings of Liberty: First Principles of the Constitution* (Lanham, MD: University Press of America, 1988), pp. 2–30.

28 "Who are the Best Keepers of the People's Liberties?" published in the *National Gazette,* 22 December 1792, in *The Papers of James Madison* 14:426.

Chapter Three

The Constitution and the Separation of Powers

"If it be a fundamental principle of free Govt. that the Legislative, Executive & Judiciary powers should be *separately* exercised; it is equally so that they be *independently* exercised."

—James Madison[1]

During the framing and ratification of the Constitution, there was no political opinion more widely accepted than that which proclaimed the separation of powers to be the foundation of constitutional government. James Madison reflected the universality of this opinion when he wrote in *The Federalist* that "[n]o political truth is certainly of greater intrinsic value, or is stamped with the authority of more enlightened patrons" than this "essential precaution in favor of liberty."[2] The framers of the Constitution were virtually unanimous in accepting Madison's statement that

> The accumulation of all powers, legislative, executive, and judiciary, in the same hands, whether of one, a few, or many, and whether hereditary, self-appointed, or elective, may justly be pronounced the very definition of tyranny (No. 47, 301).

If, indeed, the proposed Constitution did evidence a design or a tendency to such an accumulation of powers—as some Anti-Federalists alleged—Madison conceded that "no further arguments would be necessary to inspire a universal reprobation of the system" (No. 47, 301).

Whereas there was general agreement that a separation of powers was essential for the rule of law, the precise form the separated powers should assume in the new Constitution provoked vigorous debate. In the view of the leading Federalists, it was not enough to provide a negative check upon the powers of government; it was also necessary to provide for energetic government. Theophilus Parsons, in his influential *Essex Result* published in 1778, wrote that "the principles of a free republican form of government" require "modelling the three branches of the supreme power in such a manner, that the government might act with the greatest vigour and wisdom, and with the best intention." The three departments should also "retain a check upon the others, sufficient to preserve it's independence." The whole object of such modelling was, of course, to serve the leading republican principle that "no member of the state should be controlled by any law, or be deprived of his property, against his consent."[3] In a word, the separation of powers held out the prospect that constitutional government could be nontyrannical government as well as good government.

Madison and most of the leading Federalists maintained that by itself the representative principle was insufficient for preserving republican government. Although a "dependence on the people is, no doubt, the primary control on government," Madison wrote, "experience has taught mankind the necessity of auxiliary precautions" (No. 51, 322). Separation of powers, of course, is essentially a modern doctrine, one of those principles Hamilton listed as being either among "the wholly new discoveries" or those which "have made their principal progress towards perfection in modern times" (No. 9, 72).[4] Almost everyone seems to recognize, however, that the idea of the separation of powers is at least as old as Aristotle's *Politics*. Aristotle divided the functions of government into three elements: the deliberative, the magistracy, and the judicial. It is clear from Aristotle's account that the deliberative element is the predominant element of every regime. It includes many functions that would be identified today as executive or judicial. And, since Aristotle clearly implies that one institution might exercise all three functions of government, there is little indication that the separation of powers was intended to provide a checking function *among the different parts of the government*. Moreover, the predominance of the deliberative element makes it impossible for the different functions of government, even where they are exercised by different institutions, to act as a check upon the power of government.[5] As Harry Jaffa notes, "The concept of a 'power' of government is itself . . . alien to Aristotle, because our use of that expression always implies a delegation of power from a sovereign people to a government which is its instrumentality. For Aristotle, the government (*poli-*

teuma) is the regime (*politeia*) . . . "[6] The idea of a separation of state and society—in which society could make claims and limitations upon government in the name of the rights and liberties of the people—was no part of the Aristotelian scheme. The separation of state and society is a doctrine that was developed by later thinkers who had a closer relationship to the thought of the Founders.

Although the idea of the separation of powers as a constituent element of constitutional government was not unknown either to the ancients or the moderns, the version of that doctrine propounded in the American Constitution is unique in that it was intended to operate in an *unmixed* regime. As M.J.C. Vile correctly notes, "The division of functions between agencies of government who will exercise a mutual check upon each other *although both are elected, directly or indirectly, by the same people,* is a unique American contribution to modern constitutional theory."[7]

In *The Federalist* Madison wrote that "the oracle who is always consulted and cited" on the subject of the separation of powers is "the celebrated Montesquieu. If he be not the author of this invaluable precept in the science of politics, he has the merit at least of displaying and recommending it most effectually to the attention of mankind" (No. 47, 301). Indeed, Montesquieu's great work on politics, *The Spirit of the Laws,* published in 1748, was the source most cited by both proponents and opponents of the Constitution.[8] Given the weight of Montesquieu's authority, therefore, it was necessary for Madison and the Federalists to understate their disagreements—and thereby overstate their agreements—with him. Like all oracular interpretations, Madison's discussion of Montesquieu's doctrine of the separation of powers concealed as much as it revealed. *The Federalist,* I believe, presents, if not the first full-scale account of the separation of powers, then certainly the first full-scale republican account. And, if it is true, as W.B. Gwyn remarks, that the doctrine of the separation of powers had republican origins,[9] then certainly *The Federalist* must be credited with the first complete and definitive account of that doctrine.

Montesquieu's famous discussion of the separation of powers in Book XI, Chapter 6 of *The Spirit of the Laws* is brief and seems almost to be out of place in the economy of the work, since it occurs in the chapter on "The Constitution of England" but does not purport to be an accurate account of that system. At any rate, Montesquieu prefaced his remarks on the separation of powers with a definition of the "political liberty of the citizens." This is, he wrote, "a tranquility of mind arising from the opinion each person has of his safety." This tranquility is to be found "only where there is no abuse of power." And it is in the prevention of the abuse of power that the separation of powers becomes the central institution of "moderate government":

> When the legislative and executive powers are united in the same person, or in the same body of magistrates, there can be no liberty; because apprehensions may

arise, lest the same monarch or senate should enact tyrannical laws, to execute them in a tyrannical manner.

Again, there is no liberty, if the judiciary power be not separated from the legislative and executive. Were it joined with the legislative, the life and liberty of the subject would be exposed to arbitrary control; for the judge would be then the legislator. Were it joined to the executive power, the judge might behave with violence and oppression.

The Framers of the American Constitution were mindful of the fact that Montesquieu's major contribution to the separation of powers "doctrine" was the addition of an independent judiciary.

Prior to Montesquieu, the modern separation of powers theory—including that of John Locke—extended only to the legislative and executive departments; judicial power was seen as a part of executive power, the application of law in particular cases.[10] Montesquieu's attempt to distinguish judicial power seems somewhat ambiguous in that it appears to be more of an attempt to "disguise" judicial power than an attempt to distinguish it. Even though Montesquieu remarks that the power of judging is "in some sense nothing," it

ought not to be given to a standing senate; it should be exercised by persons taken from the body of the people at certain times of the year, and consistently with a form and manner prescribed by law, in order to erect a tribunal that should last only so long as necessity requires. By this method the power of judging, *so terrible to mankind,* not being annexed to any particular state or profession, becomes, as it were, *invisible and nothing.* People have not then the judges continually present to their view; they fear the office, but not the magistrate (XI, 6).

This power of judging was to be exercised by juries drawn periodically from the people, and in the exercise of the jury function the people were themselves to be judges. Juries would continually emerge from the people and then dissolve back into the mass of society. It was this aspect of constituting the judicial power that made it "invisible and nothing." Since no magistrate exercised this "terrible power" directly, its influence would thereby be almost "invisible." It remained for the Framers of the American Constitution to complete the establishment of an independent judicial power by transforming Montesquieu's jury system into a judiciary and juries into judges.

The principal reason that Montesquieu's doctrine of the separation of powers was in need of modification, however, was that it rested on the mixed regime principle. As Thomas Pangle notes, "Montesquieu still believed that the competition which keeps powers limited requires a real class division among the citizenry."[11] Like Locke before him, Montesquieu sought to distribute the powers of government among different classes—monarchy, aristocracy, and democracy. The legislative function was to be divided between the democracy and an hereditary nobility with the executive branch held by the monarchy. The natural class antagonisms that pre-existed in society would thus be reflected on the level of government, preventing one class from dominating the government.

This balanced or mixed government would provide the stability or moderation necessary for the rule of law and prevent government from becoming too powerful. It was therefore not a system that looked primarily to the protection of the rights and liberties of individuals, but the protection of the rights and liberties of the various classes. Montesquieu may have alluded to this when he wrote that "the three powers can be well distributed with regard to the liberty of the constitution, although they are not so well distributed with regard to the liberty of the citizen" (XI, 18). As Martin Diamond correctly noted, "the mixed regime was . . . defended, partly, as a barrier against oppression by one class of another—not, be it noted, as a protection of the liberties of individuals—and it was further defended, even more importantly, on the ground that by bringing together two partial conceptions of justice, statesmanship could hope to achieve a complete justice by harmonizing these opposing conceptions. Thus, in the mixed regime, rival claims regarding justice were in the very structure of the system."[12] For Montesquieu, constitutional government—and hence the rule of law—was rooted in the class-based structure of society itself. Without this agency, it would be impossible to contrive an effective separation of powers because there would be no "rival claims regarding justice" among an undivided people that could serve as the source of the checking function that the separation of powers was designed to provide.

This class structure was, of course, lacking in America. There was no hereditary nobility and no prospect of creating one. Indeed, the Constitution's prohibition against the creation of titles of nobility was considered to be "the cornerstone of republican government," because, Hamilton wrote in *The Federalist,* as long as titles of nobility are "excluded there can never be serious danger that the government will be any other than that of the people" (No. 84, 512). Almost everyone recognized that a class-based constitutional arrangement was contrary to the "genius of the American people." Several delegates to the Constitutional Convention noted the inappositeness of predicating a separation of powers upon class. Charles Pinkney, for example, remarked that, although he believed the "Constitution of G. Britain" to be the best in existence,

> it might easily be shown that the peculiar excellence, the distinguishing feature of that Governm[en]t, can not possibly be introduced into our System—that its balance between the Crown & people can not be made a part of our Constitution—that we neither have or can have the members to compose it, nor the rights, privileges & properties of so distinct a class of Citizens to guard—that the materials for forming this balance or check do not exist.[13]

It was thus necessary to find a republican substitute for the mixed regime principle. This substitute was found in the constitutional system of checks and balances, and in the manner in which all the powers of government were derived, in the words of *The Federalist,* "directly or indirectly from the great body of the people" (No. 39, 241). It was, of course, a task of particular delicacy to determine the precise configuration the constitutional system was to assume, and it was here that the bulk of the debate over the separation of powers took place during the founding period.

In *The Federalist,* Madison noted that one of the "principal objections" levied against the Constitution "by the more respectable adversaries" was that it had so blended and intermingled the powers of government as "to expose some of the essential parts of the edifice to the danger of being crushed by the disproportionate weight of other parts" (No. 47, 301). An Officer of the Late Continental Army expressed a widely held Anti-Federalist opinion when he wrote that "The LEGISLATIVE and EXECUTIVE powers are not kept separate as every one of the American constitutions declares they ought to be; but they are mixed in a manner entirely novel and unknown, even to the constitution of Great Britain."[14] Cincinatus wrote in a similar vein, citing Montesquieu and DeLolme as his authority: "it would have been proper, not only to have previously laid down, in a declaration of rights, that these powers should be forever separate and incommunicable; but the frame of the proposed constitution, should have had that separation religiously in view, through all its parts. It is manifest this was not the object of its framers, but, that on the contrary there is a studied mixture of them."[15] And Federal Farmer, who conceded the necessity of some mixing and balancing of the powers of government, nevertheless contended that the particular admixture represented in the Constitution had a dangerous tendency toward the accumulation of executive power. Republican government, he maintained, did not need such a complicated system of checks and balances: "Where the members of the government, as the house, the senate, the executive, and judiciary, are strong and complete, each in itself, the balance is naturally produced, each party may take the powers congenial to it, and we have less need to be anxious about checks, and the subdivision of powers."[16]

In part, the argument was over the issue of complex versus simple government. The genius of republican government was always thought to reside in its simplicity. Republican liberty does not need complex and complicated government for its security; complexity merely allows potential despots to disguise their ambitions. This was the argument that animated the Anti-Federalist support for small republicanism. Large republics, the Anti-Federalists argued, are necessarily complex governments and therefore will inevitably become despotic. The mixed (and complex) system contemplated in the Constitution would, Federal Farmer alleged, establish a dangerous "new species of executive."[17]

What Madison understood, and the Anti-Federalists did not, was that checks and balances, entailing the extensive sharing of constitutional power, were made necessary by the republican principle itself, a principle that did not give constitutional status or recognition to class. Checks and balances, of course, are superfluous in a mixed regime. It is not necessary to contrive defensive mechanisms for the different branches of government because those defenses will be supplied by the competing class interests. The Anti-Federalists interpreted Montesquieu's "pure theory" of the separation of powers as if it had been intended for a republic rather than a mixed regime. Madison thus had to modify Montesquieu to make his "doctrine" of the separation of powers compatible with the principles of an "unmixed" regime.

> [I]t may clearly be inferred that Montesquieu could not have meant that the legislative, executive, and judiciary ought to have no *partial agency* in, or no *control* over, the acts of each other. His meaning, as his own words import, . . . can amount to no more than this, that where the *whole* power of one department is exercised by the same hands which possess the *whole* power of another department, the fundamental principles of a free constitution are subverted (No. 47, 302–303; see 401, 483).[18]

The Anti-Federalists rigorously held to the traditional view that the principal purpose of the separation of powers was to augment legislative power against the prerogatives of executive power. They were never able to reconcile themselves to the idea of energetic government—energy and liberty were simply irreconcilable. Liberty could exist only within the interstices of the *exceptions* to sovereign power, never in its vigorous exercise, however well constructed government might be to control the abuse of power. But since the new form of government contemplated the sovereignty of the people with the government possessing only those powers delegated by the people, the Federalists maintained that the calculus of separated powers had changed. Executive power now had to be augmented to serve as a check against the prerogatives of legislative power.

The Anti-Federalist reliance on legislative power was connected to the small republic argument of Montesquieu. Centinel proclaimed "the form of government, which holds those entrusted with power, in the greatest responsibility to their constituents, the best calculated for freemen. A republican, or free government, can only exist where the body of the people are virtuous, and where property is pretty equally divided; in such a government the people are the sovereign and their sense or opinion is the criterion of every public measure; for when this ceases to be the case, the nature of the government is changed, and an aristocracy, monarch or despotism will rise on its ruin."[19] Citing Montesquieu as his authority, Centinel concluded that "it will not be controverted that the legislative is the highest delegated power in government, and that all others are subordinate to it."[20] According to Federal Farmer, a "fair representation" of the people was therefore the essential guarantee of republican principle. "A full and equal representation, is that which possesses the same interests, feelings, opinions, and views the people themselves would were they all assembled—a fair representation, therefore, should be so regulated, that every order of men in the community, according to the common course of elections, can have a share in it."[21]

With a virtuous citizenry there is little need for complicated schemes of separated powers because the principle of representation itself will insure the enactment of just policies. But as *The Federalist* countered, not only is this argument for proportional representation "altogether visionary" (No. 35, 214), it also fails to account for the possibility that legislative power itself could be a source of danger to republican liberty. A virtuous citizenry may be necessary for republican government, but, as Hamilton argued in the New York ratifying convention, it is also necessary to rely on "auxiliary" institutions that connect "the virtue of . . . rulers with their interest." And once the principle of separation is conceded to be necessary to republican government, it is no longer possible to adhere to the proposition that republican government must be simple government. As Hamilton continued his description of the new Constitution, he remarked that "in the form of this government . . . you find all the checks which the greatest politicians and the best writers have ever conceived. . . . The organization is so complex, so skillfully contrived, that it is next to impossible that an impolitic or wicked measure should pass the scrutiny with success."[22]

The Anti-Federalist view was represented in most of the state constitutions prior to 1787. Charles Thatch accurately described the situation when he wrote that "in actual operation, these first state constitutions produced what was tantamount to legislative omnipotence. . . . Separation of powers, whatever formal adherence was given the principle in bills of rights, meant the subordinate executive carrying out the legislative will."[23] The example of the state governments was a great concern to the members of the Constitutional Convention.[24] James Wilson inquired: "Is there no danger of a Legislative despotism? Theory & practice both proclaim it. If the legislative authority be not restrained, there can be neither liberty nor stability."[25]

The state constitutions contained strong commitments to separation of powers. The Massachusetts constitution of 1780 is typical:

> In the government of this Commonwealth, the legislative department shall never exercise the executive and judicial powers, or either of them: The executive shall never exercise the legislative and judicial powers, or either of them: The judicial shall never exercise the legislative and executive powers, or either of them: to the end it may be a government of laws and not of men.

But the framers of the state constitutions did not take adequate measures to establish in practice what they conceded to be necessary in theory. As Madison remarked in *The Federalist*, "in no instance has a competent provision been made for maintaining in practice the separation delineated on paper." The principal reason for this, according to Madison, was that "The founders of our republics . . . seem never for a moment to have turned their eyes from the danger, to liberty, from the overgrown and all-grasping prerogative of an hereditary magistrate, supported and fortified by an hereditary branch of the legislative authority. They seem never to have recollected the danger from legislative usurpations, which, by assembling all power in the same hands, must lead to the same tyranny as is threatened by executive usurpations" (No. 48, 309).

In a republic there is no analogy between the power of a monarch and the power of an elected magistrate—a powerful executive was not, as many opponents of energetic government claimed, "the foetus of monarchy."[26] In a monarchy, executive power is indeed the source of danger. But in a republic, where the executive is carefully limited and the legislature "is inspired by a supposed influence over the people" and possesses "an intrepid confidence in its own strength," the legislature possesses a natural advantage over the other branches. It is against the "enterprising ambition" of the legislative department, Madison concludes, "that the people ought to indulge all their jealousy and exhaust all their precautions" (No. 48, 309). The particular danger of legislative supremacy to republicanism is that the legislature is the natural representative of majority faction, the disease "most incident to republican government" (No. 10, 84). The principal defect of the state governments was not, of course, their lack of an effective separation of powers, but the smallness and lack of diversity that allowed their legislatures to be dominated by majority factions. Separation of powers is only an "auxiliary" consideration.

In *The Federalist,* Madison describes the two-fold character of an effective separation of powers: first, it is necessary to discriminate "in theory, the several classes of power, as they may in their nature be legislative, executive, or judiciary"; the second and "most difficult task" is to devise a means of providing "some practical security for each, against the invasion of the others" (No. 48, 308). It is significant that Madison does not say here that the theoretical discrimination of the various powers according to their nature is an easy task, only that providing "practical security" is the "most difficult." The reason is that he had already made the case for the difficulty of the classification of the various powers according to their nature.

> Experience has instructed us that no skill in the science of government has yet been able to discriminate and define, with sufficient certainty, its three great provinces—the legislative, executive, and judiciary; or even the privileges and powers of the different legislative branches. Questions daily occur in the course of practice which prove the obscurity which reigns in these subjects, and which puzzle the greatest adepts in political science (No. 37, 228).

We learn in *The Federalist* No. 51 that the task of providing "practical security" consists "in giving to those who administer each department the necessary constitutional means and personal motives to resist encroachments of the others" (No. 51, 321–322). The "constitutional means" comprise the various modes of mixing and interblending the different powers of government that we have come to know as checks and balances. The argument for checks and balances, then, depends, in no small measure, on the fact that there is some indistinctness in the nature of the powers to be separated. The fact that by nature the powers are indistinct makes it appear that their combination can also be natural. If there were no possibility of mixing and interblending the legislative, executive, and judicial powers consistently with the principles of republican government, there would be no possibility of an effective separation in practice. As Madison remarks, "unless these departments be so far connected and blended as to give to each a constitutional control over the others, the degree of separation which the maxim requires, as essential to a free government, can never in practice be duly maintained" (No. 48, 308). The "great problem to be solved," then is not a theoretical one, but a practical one; or at least it is a problem in which nature (the indistinct nature of the powers to be separated) lends itself fully to the support of practice. We would not add, however, that this is an instance where it is necessary for practice to inform theory.

Unlike many of the state constitutions, nothing in the Constitution directly mandates a separation of powers. Rather its existence is inferred from the fact that the three branches of government are detailed in separate articles. A comparison of the language of the three articles is revealing. Congress is entrusted with "All legislative Powers *herein granted*" (Art. I, sec. 1), whereas the president is charged with "The executive Power" (Art. II, sec. 1), and the Judiciary with "The judicial Power of the United States" (Art. III, sec. 1). The implication is that the president will exercise "the executive power" limited only by specific constitutional restrictions, whereas Congress is limited to the exercise of specifically granted powers. Significantly, Congress is not charged with exercising the "legislative power of the United States." It is also not unworthy of notice that the president is the only officer of government required by the Constitution to take an oath of office not only to defend and preserve the Constitution but also to execute faithfully the office of the president.

Article II does detail specific executive functions. The argument has been made that if the president were indeed given the power to exercise more generalized "executive power", a listing of the specific powers would have been superfluous. Thus, the only way to read the Constitution so as not to make the specific list of powers superfluous is to read them—as in the case of Congress' powers—as an exhaustive list of specific grants of power, not as a generalized command to exercise executive power. Hamilton supplied an adequate answer to this interpretation in 1793 in his Pacificus essays. "It would not consist with the rules of sound construction," Hamilton wrote, "to consider this enumeration of particular authorities as derogating from the more comprehensive grant in the general clause, further than as it may be coupled with express restrictions or limitations." Thus, Hamilton continued, "The enumeration ought therefore to be considered as intended by way of greater caution, to specify and regulate the principal articles implied in the definition of Executive Power; leaving the rest to flow from the general grant of that power, interpreted in conformity with other parts of the Constitution, and with the principles of free government."[27] From Hamilton's point of view—and I daresay this was the point of view of the Framers generally—the bulwark of a limited constitution resided in the fact that Congress' powers were specifically enumerated, not in the limitation of executive or judicial power.

Practice, however, requires something more than mere "parchment barriers"—a delineation of the boundaries of the powers of government without specific measures to ensure separation in practice. Yet, this is the "security which appears to have been principally relied upon by the compilers of most the American constitutions." Parchment barriers will be inadequate to resist "the encroaching spirit of power" by the "more powerful members of the government" against the "more feeble." And as Madison was fond of remarking, "the legislative department is everywhere extending the sphere of its activity and drawing all power into its impetuous vortex" (No. 48, 309).[28] The predominance of the legislative branch is natural in any popular form of government; it results from the fact that the legislature is the most immediate representative of sovereign power, the people. It derives advantages from other sources as well: besides the fact that the legislature will have exclusive "access to the pockets of the people," it has "constitutional powers . . . at once more extensive and less susceptible of precise limits." From this latter circumstance, "it can, with the greater facility, mask under complicated and indirect measures, the encroachments which it makes on the co-ordinate departments" (No. 48, 310).

It is not possible, however, "to give to each department an equal power of self-defense." Since the "legislative authority necessarily predominates" in republican government, this "inconveniency" is met by dividing the legislature into rival branches. The "weakness of the executive may require, on the other hand, that it should be fortified." The "natural defense" appears "at first view" to be an absolute veto. The absolute veto, however, may be inconsistent with the principles of republican government; more importantly, an absolute negative might not be as frequently exercised as the qualified veto. The nature of republican government, and the necessity of an energetic executive, seems therefore to require the qualified veto. (No. 51, 322–323). The other "constitutional means" possessed by the executive, such as the power to propose legislation, the appointment of judges, and the power of pardon, are designed to fortify the executive branch against the legislative. This scheme of checks and balances is designed to make the different branches independent, so that independence can serve as the means of defense for the weaker branches against the stronger. Throughout the construction of the executive branch, the principle that guided the Framers of the Constitution was to combine, "as far as republican principles will admit, all the requisites to energy" (No. 77, 463).

This principle is well illustrated by Hamilton's discussion of the treaty power. Acknowledging that objections had been made on the ground of "the trite topic of the intermixture of powers," Hamilton defends the Convention's decision to place the treaty-making power in the executive "by and with the advice and consent of the Senate." Hamilton remarks that "the particular nature of the power of making treaties indicates a peculiar propriety in the union." The nature of this power, Hamilton maintains, is more legislative than executive, "though it does not seem strictly to fall within the definition of either of them." The "objects" of treaty-making "are CONTRACTS with foreign nations which have the force of law, but derive it from the obligations of good faith. They are not rules prescribed by the sovereign to the subject, but agreements between sovereign and sovereign. The power in question seems therefore to form a distinct department" (No. 75, 450–451).

Hamilton here alludes to Locke's distinction between "federative power" and "executive power." The federative power, according to Locke, is concerned with "all the Transactions, with all Persons and Communities without the Commonwealth" and is therefore "much less capable to be directed by antecedent, standing, positive Laws, than the Executive; and so must necessarily be left to the Prudence and Wisdom of those whose hands it is in, to be managed for the public good."[29] Locke calls this "Federative" power "natural," because it corresponds "to the Power every Man naturally had before he entered into Society."[30] Even though the executive and federative powers are by nature distinct, "they are always almost united" in the same person. But, as Hamilton admits, the republican principle demands that federative power—at least insofar as it involves treaty-making—be divided between the executive and the Senate. To have entrusted the power of making treaties solely to the president would have been "utterly unsafe and improper."

> The history of human conduct does not warrant that exalted opinion of human virtue which would make it wise in a nation to commit interests of so delicate and momentous a kind, as those which concern its intercourse with the rest of the world, to the sole disposal of a magistrate created and circumstanced as would be a President of the United States (No. 75, 451).

Entrusting the treaty-making power solely to the Senate, in contrast, "would have been to relinquish the benefits of the constitutional agency of the President in the conduct of foreign negotiations." The union of the treaty-making power in the executive and the Senate is thus made necessary by the nature of the powers involved and the nature of republican principles.

There were several proposals at the Constitutional Convention to have the president elected by the legislature. But, as James Wilson argued, such a mode of selecting the executive would render it "too dependent to stand as the mediator between the intrigues & sinister view of the Representatives and the general liberties & interests of the people."[31] Wilson's view was seconded by Gouverneur Morris who charged that "If the Executive be chosen by the Natl' Legislature, he will not be independent of it; and if not independent, usurpation & tyranny on the part of the Legislature will be the consequence."[32] The leading architects of Article II were well aware of the fact that, in Hamilton's terms, "energy in the executive is the leading character in the very definition of good government" (No. 70, 423).

In the Constitutional Convention, Madison failed in his attempt to persuade the delegates to adopt another "auxiliary precaution" that he regarded as essential in translating the theory of separation into secure practice, a Council of Revision. This Council would have been composed of the executive and a specified number of Supreme Court justices. Its function would have been to provide a "Revisionary check on the Legislature" through the prior review of legislative proposals. It would, Madison argued, provide a defensive mechanism against "Legislative encroachments" for both the executive and judicial branches. Madison regarded the defeat of the revisory Council and his failure to secure a national veto on state legislation as his two greatest defeats in the Convention. The Council was rejected because many delegates believed that this intermixture would violate the separation of powers, primarily because it would give the judiciary a double check on legislative power, once as part of the revisory power and again in the normal course of judicial review of legislation. James Wilson countered this contention, arguing that the Council would give the Court a proper role in policy determination.

> It had been said that the Judges, as expositors of the Laws would have an opportunity of defending their constitutional rights. There was weight in this observation; but this power of the Judges did not go far enough. Laws may be unjust, may be unwise, may be dangerous, may be destructive; and yet not be so unconstitutional as to justify the Judges in refusing to give them effect. Let them have a share in the Revisionary power, and they will have an opportunity of taking notice of these characters of a law . . . "[33]

A majority of the Convention reasoned that such a mixture would make "statesmen of the Judges," thus setting them up—instead of the legislature—as the guardians of the rights of the people. Most delegates seemed to believe that republicanism demanded that the judiciary not be involved in policymaking, because policymaking entails more than the exercise of judgment. There is, of course, some question as to whether the Council would have genuinely contributed to executive independence, or whether it would have only served to strengthen judicial power at the expense of executive power. In the latter case, the Council would have failed to provide an effective check on legislative omnipotence.

The natural superiority of the legislative branch also made it necessary for the Framers to construct an independent judiciary. A "complete independence of the courts of justice," Hamilton wrote in *The Federalist,* was necessary to insure the legislature's—and the people's—adherence to the Constitution in those instances where it is inspired by an intrepid sense of its own strength to ignore the Supreme Law of the land. An independent judiciary is therefore necessary in order to place the courts in the role "as the bulwarks of a limited Constitution against legislative encroachments" (No. 78, 466). This is the main reason that the independence of the judiciary depends on the permanent tenure of judges, which "must soon destroy all sense of dependence on the authority conferring" the appointments (No. 51, 321). Richard Epstein remarks that "The judiciary is on a long leash at the edge of the strictly republican regime, reflecting the hope that good government can promise repose and tranquility to every individual man."[34] The only thing that saves the judiciary from being that un-republican, "will independent of society" that Madison warns against in *The Federalist* No. 51, is that fact that the judiciary has no will—only judgment (No. 51, 323; No. 78, 465).

This independence does not, however, "suppose a superiority of the judicial to the legislative power. It only supposes that the power of the people is superior to both, and that where the will of the legislature, declared in its statutes, stands in opposition to that of the people, declared in the Constitution, the judges ought to be governed by fundamental laws rather than by those which are not fundamental" (No. 78, 468). This idea of an independent judiciary received its greatest explication in Chief Justice Marshall's opinion in *Marbury v. Madison* (1803). But Marshall was careful to note, in a passage that Hamilton surely would have applauded, that "[t]he province of this court is, solely, to decide on the rights of individuals, not to enquire how the executive, or executive officers, perform duties in which they have a discretion. Questions, in their nature political, or which are, by the constitution and laws, submitted to the executive, can never be made in this court."[35]

There is some doubt, however, whether the Framers of the Constitution or Marshall would endorse the present-day version of judicial review. Today's version casts the Supreme Court in the role "as ultimate interpreter of the Constitution" in all matters involving the separation of powers.[36] This notion of judicial supremacy renders the Court too prone at times to confuse the Constitution with constitutional law. The Supreme Court has gone so far as to imply— supposedly relying on Marshall's argument in *Marbury*—that its *interpretations* of the Constitution are "the Supreme Law of the Land."[37] Marshall, however, had rightly argued that "the framers of the constitution contemplated that instrument as a rule for the government of courts, as well as of the legislature."[38]

In addition to providing the necessary "constitutional means" for maintaining the independence of the branches of government, it is also essential to provide the requisite "personal motives." For, without personal motives, there is the danger that government will not be energetic, that those who occupy the various constitutional offices will not employ the "constitutional means" of independence that are attached to their office. In a mixed regime, the motives for independence are provided by the rival claims and interests of the different classes in society. Republican government must replace class motives with personal ones. Madison remarks that "ambition must be made to counteract ambition. The interest of the man must be connected with the constitutional rights of the place." It is in this manner that interest and public spiritedness are combined so that "the private interest of every individual may be a sentinel over the public rights." These are in some sense, Madison laconically remarks, "inventions of prudence" (No. 51, 322).

The great problem in arranging a separation of powers in a popular government is in devising a method of introducing different interests into the government. Discussing the Virginia Constitution in the *Notes on the State of Virginia,* Jefferson noted that "The senate is, by its constitution, too homogeneous with the house of delegates. Being chosen by the same electors, at the same time, and out of the same subjects, the choice falls of course on men of the same description . . . We do not therefore derive from the separation of our legislature into two houses, those benefits which a proper complication of principles is capable of producing." The result is that "All the powers of government, legislative, executive and judiciary, result to the legislative body," thus forming an "elective despotism."[39] The Constitution supplies "a proper complication of principles" by the use of differing modes of election. By deriving power from the people by means of different channels—directly or indirectly—different interests can be introduced into the level of government and serve as the basis for the ambitions and personal motives of those who occupy the various offices. Hamilton spoke of this as "the dissimilar modes of constituting the several component parts of the government. The House of Representatives' being to be elected immediately by the people, the Senate by the State legislatures, the President by electors chosen for that purpose by the people, there would be little probability of a common interest to cement these different branches in predilection for any particular class of electors" (No. 60, 368).

The Senate, for example, is ultimately responsible to the majority of society, but it is a different majority than the one that elects both the House of Representatives and the president; and the different branches are not only responsible to majorities derived in different ways but majorities formed at different times. Presumably, in a large, diverse republic, majorities formed at different intervals will express different views and interests. With these "transient" majorities being the most characteristic feature of modern republicanism, the government is free to represent the public good.

The Federalist's explication of the separation of powers proceeds in terms of interest and ambition rather than virtue. As Hamilton wrote, the "best security for the fidelity of mankind is to make their interest coincide with their duty. Even the love of fame, the ruling passion of the noblest minds," would be insufficient for ensuring an energetic executive where there is no immediate prospect for enhancing one's reputation (No. 72, 437). The language of interest does not deny the possibility—or even the necessity—of virtue or public spiritedness. But *The Federalist* is "disposed to view human nature as it is, without either flattering its virtues or exaggerating its vices . . . " (No. 76, 458). There is no doubt that the Framers placed ultimate reliance on the "genius of the people of America" for the success of the experiment in republicanism. The honor of human nature—"the principles of the Revolution"—demanded such reliance. But the Framers were always mindful of the necessity of "auxiliary" precautions to account for the "ordinary depravity of human nature" (No. 78, 471).

Republican government in which the separation of powers is to be the practical guarantee of liberty must be energetic government. But as some observers have pointed out, the term "energy"—in 1787 only recently imported into political discourse from physics—is neutral with respect to forms of government. An energetic executive can be either a monarch or a republican executive. And, as Harvey Mansfield has recently written, "if energy is not virtue, in the American Constitution it leads to virtue. In Publius' argument we see a progression from the neutrality of energy as it answers the necessities that any government must face to the indispensable contribution energy makes to the goodness of republican government."[40] With a properly constructed government energy can be the source of republican virtue. Without the proper constitutional forms the connection between energy and virtue will be less certain.

The great object of republican statesmanship is to insure not only that government will be energetic, but also that the objects of ambition are the objects worthy of "the noblest minds." The love of fame partakes of the same neutrality as "energy." As Abraham Lincoln pointed out in his Lyceum Speech in 1838, "Towering genius disdains a beaten path. . . . It thirsts and burns for distinction; and, if possible, it will have it, whether at the expense of emancipating slaves, or enslaving freemen."[41] When such a genius springs up in the midst of self-governing society, Lincoln noted, it will require a united people attached to the Constitution and the laws to be able to frustrate his designs.

Since energy and ambition are ambiguous springs to public spiritedness, the structure of government must be designed to insure that both will be directed to the public good. This is the reason that "ambition must be made to counteract ambition" (No. 51, 322). The honor and ambition of those who occupy the constitutional offices will be served only when the nation prospers. Thus it is not so much the virtue of the rulers as the virtue of constitutional forms that insures the public good. The noblest minds will not be the product of a noble class. The various constitutional offices will be open to talent, but those who occupy the offices will not be the products of talented classes—their motives will be personal, not derived from class interests. The argument for virtue, which is not entirely absent from *The Federalist,* would imply the necessity of virtuous classes or an aristocracy. Virtue is thus never an explicit theme of *The Federalist*. The people will choose those who are most qualified for office, and their virtue—and perhaps their spiritedness—will be reflected in those whom they elect. Madison made this illuminating remark in the Virginia ratifying convention: "I go on this great republican principle, that the people will have virtue and intelligence to select men of virtue and wisdom. . . . If there be sufficient virtue and intelligence in the community, it will be exercised in the selection of these men; so that we do not depend on their virtue, or put confidence in our rulers, but in the people who are to choose them."[42]

As Mansfield notes, "the people, whose interest is to elect rather than rule, must have the virtue to appreciate virtue and the judgment to trust it. But when they elect the constitutional officers, their virtue is not, or does not appear to them as, deferring to greater virtue."[43] No doubt, as Mansfield suggests, elections flatter the people's pretense to rule with the illusion of rule. But as Madison makes clear, democratic flattery is a double-edged sword: "those ties which bind the representative to his constituents are strengthened by motives of a more selfish nature. His pride and vanity attach him to a form of government which favors his pretensions and gives him a share in its honors and distinctions" (No. 57, 352). Republics can invite the ambitious to fill their constitutional offices because there are constitutional devices—most particularly the separation of powers, which has now received its principal perfection in the American Constitution—to insure that however ambitious rulers might be, they will be confronted not only by the ambitious of other constitutional officers, but ultimately by the ambition of the people. The people's ambitions are derived from the "manly spirit" of the Revolution, a spirit "which actuates the people of America—a spirit which nourishes freedom, and in return is nourished by it" (No. 14, 104; No. 57, 353). This ultimate ground of republican government and all other considerations—however important they may be—are merely auxiliary.

NOTES

1   Max Farrand, ed., *The Records of the Federal Convention of 1787,* 4 vols. (New Haven: Yale University Press, 1966), 2:56.
2   *The Federalist* No. 47, ed. Clinton Rossiter (New York: 1961), 301. Further references to the *The Federalist* appear in the text by number and page.
3   Charles S. Hyneman and Donald S. Lutz, eds., *American Political Writings During the Founding Era, 1760–1805,* 2 vols. (Indianapolis: Liberty Press, 1983), 1:521.
4   The Anti-Federalist Centinel, although maintaining that "the highest responsibility is to be attained in a simple structure of government," nonetheless concurred with Hamilton, calling the separation of powers "the chief improvement in government in modern times." Herbert Storing, ed., *The Complete Anti-Federalist,* 7 vols. (Chicago: University of Chicago Press, 1981), 2.7.9; 2.7.50; see also Rawlins Lowndes, in ibid., 5.13.7. Martin Diamond, "The Separation of Powers and the Mixed Regime," *Publius* 8 (Summer 1978), p. 33, remarks that "The separation of powers is a modern invention and its modernity is decisive to its understanding. The American Founders understood that modernity well."
5   See Aristotle, *Politics,* Bk. IV, Ch. 14, 1296b16 ff.

6 Harry V. Jaffa, "What is Politics? An Interpretation of Aristotle's *Politics*," in *The Conditions of Freedom: Essays in Political Philosophy* (Baltimore: Johns Hopkins University Press, 1975), p. 64.

7 M.J.C. Vile, *Constitutionalism and the Separation of Powers* (Oxford: Clarendon Press, 1967), p. 125; cf. pp. 122, 134.

8 Donald Lutz, "The Relative Influence of European Writers on Late Eighteenth-Century American Political Thought," *American Political Science Review* 78 (March 1984), p. 189.

9 W.B. Gwyn, *The Meaning of the Separation of Powers* (New Orleans: Tulane University Press, 1965), p. 27 "the earliest proponents of the separation of powers were republicans . . . "

10 Gwyn, pp. 100–102. As late as 1776, a writer in Philadelphia remarked that "Government is generally distinguished into three parts, Executive, Legislative and Judicial; but this is more a distinction of words than things . . . the distinction is perplexing, and however we may refine and define, there is no more than two powers in any government, viz. the power to make laws, and the power to execute them; for the judicial power is only a branch of the executive." *American Political Writings During the Founding Era, 1760–1805,* 1:387.

11 Thomas Pangle, *Montesquieu's Philosophy of Liberalism* (Chicago: University of Chicago Press, 1973), p. 125. See Vile, p. 93; Gwyn, pp. 104, 110.

12 Diamond, "The Separation of Powers and the Mixed Regime," p. 36.

13 Farrand, *Records of the Federal Convention of 1787,* 1:398; see 1:87, 101, 153.

14 Storing, *The Complete Anti-Federalist,* 3.8.3.

15 Ibid., 6.1.33.

16 Ibid., 2.8.175; see Brutus, 2.9.197.

17 Ibid., 2.8.22.

18 See Charles C. Thach, *The Creation of the Presidency, 1775–1789* (Baltimore: Johns Hopkins University Press, 1923 [reprinted 1969]), pp. 169, 95. "The framers of the Constitution" were not "content to accept [Montesquieu's] political abstraction on its own merits and then apply it blindly.

19 Storing, *The Complete Anti-Federalist,* 2.7.9.

20 Ibid., 2.7.11.

21 Ibid., 2.8.15; see 2.8.39, 2.8.96–97, 2.8.156.

22 Johnathan Elliot, ed., *Debates in the Several State Conventions on the Federal Constitution,* 5 vols., 2nd ed. (Philadelphia: Lippincott, 1836–1845), 2:348.

23 *The Creation of the Presidency,* pp. 34; 41, 42–43. "Whatever the theory, there was legislative omnipotence . . . The legislature was sovereign."

24 See Madison, "Vices of the Political System of the U[nited] States," in Robert A. Rutland and Charles F. Hobson, eds., *The Papers of James Madison,* 16 vols. to date (Chicago: University of Chicago Press; Charlottesville: University Press of Virginia, 1962–   ), 9:353–357.

25 Farrand, *The Records of the Federal Convention of 1787,* 1:254; see 1:26–27, 1:86, 1:203, 2:30, 2:35, 2:76.

26 Ibid., 1:66. The statement is by Edmund Randolph.

27 Alexander Hamilton, "Pacificus No. 1," in Harold C. Syrett, et al., eds., *The Papers of Alexander Hamilton,* 26 vols. (New York: Columbia University Press, 1961–1978), 15:39.

28 See Farrand, *Records of the Federal Convention of 1787,* 2:35.
29 *Second Treatise on Government,* in Peter Laslett, ed., *Two Treatises of Government* (New York: New American Library, 1965), par. 147.
30 Ibid., par. 145.
31 Farrand, *Records of the Federal Convention of 1787,* 2:30.
32 Ibid., 2:31; see also 2:109, 300–301, 403.
33 Ibid., 2:73.
34 *The Political Theory of The Federalist* (Chicago: University of Chicago Press, 1984), p. 192.
35 *Marbury v. Madison,* 5 U.S. (1 Cranch) 137, 170 (1803).
36 *Baker v. Carr,* 369 U.S. 186, 211 (1962).
37 *Cooper v. Aaron,* 358 U.S. 1 (1958).
38 *Marbury,* at 179–180. See Erler, "Judicial Legislation" in Leonard Levy and Kenneth Karst, eds., *The Encyclopedia of the American Constitution,* 4 vols. (New York: Macmillan, 1986), 3:1040.
39 *Notes on the State of Virginia,* Query XIII, in Merrill D. Peterson, ed., *Jefferson: Writings* (New York: Library of America, 1984), p. 245.
40 Harvey Mansfield, Jr., "Republicanizing the Executive," in Charles R. Kesler, ed., *Saving the Revolution: The Federalist Papers and the American Founding* (New York: The Free Press, 1987), p. 178.
41 Roy P. Basler, ed., *The Collected Works of Abraham Lincoln,* 9 vols. (New Brunswick, NJ: Rutgers University Press, 1953), 1:114.
42 *Debates in the Several State Conventions on the Federal Constitution,* 3:536–537.
43 Mansfield, "Republicanizing the Executive," p. 184.

Chapter Four

The Separation of Powers in the Administrative State

"But because those Laws which are constantly to be Executed, and whose force is always to continue, may be made in little time; therefore there is no need, that the *Legislative* should be always in being, not having always business to do. And because it may be too great a temptation to humane frailty apt to grasp at Power, for the same Persons who have the Power of making Laws, to have also in their hands the power to execute them, whereby they may exempt themselves from Obedience to the Laws they make, and suit the Law, both in its making and execution, to their own private advantage, and thereby come to have a distinct interest from the rest of the Community, contrary to end of Society and Government."

—John Locke[1]

"If there is a principle in our Constitution, indeed in any free Constitution more sacred than another, it is that which separates the legislative, executive and judicial powers. If there is any point in which the separation of the legislative and executive powers ought to be maintained with great caution, it is that which relates to officers and offices."

—James Madison[2]

Throughout American history, the separation of powers doctrine has indeed been held almost as a "sacred principle" of constitutional government. There have been, of course, many disputes about the precise configuration of the separated powers[3] but rarely any doubts about the efficacy of the principle itself. Today, however, the principle is vigorously challenged in the name of efficient government—or more precisely, in the name of the administrative state. As one political scientist has remarked, "[t]he fundamental problem, in trying to make the government of the United States work effectively, is not to preserve the separation of powers but to overcome it. For anything of consequence to be accomplished, the executive and legislative branches must be brought from confrontation into a reasonable degree of harmony . . . [C]onfrontation, stalemate and deadlock . . . frequently leave the government of the United States impotent to cope with complex problems."[4]

In 1926, Justice Louis Brandeis could still remark that "[t]he doctrine of the separation of powers was adopted by the Convention of 1787 not to promote efficiency but to preclude the exercise of arbitrary power. The purpose was not to avoid friction, but, by means of the inevitable friction incident to the distribution of the governmental powers among three departments, to save the people from autocracy."[5] At the very time Brandeis wrote these lines, however, powerful forces of the Progressive movement had long been advocating the abolition of the separation of powers as an obstacle to effective leadership and efficient administration. Woodrow Wilson, the intellectual leader of the Progressives, wrote in his *Congressional Government,* first published in 1885, that "[a]s at present constituted, the federal government lacks strength because its powers are divided, lacks promptness because its authorities are multiplied, lacks wieldiness because its processes are roundabout, lacks efficiency because its responsibility is indistinct and its action without competent direction."[6]

The theory of the separation of powers, according to Wilson, was the product of an age that placed its trust in the mechanistic universe of Newtonian physics. "The makers of our federal Constitution," Wilson wrote in his 1908 treatise *Constitutional Government,*

> followed the scheme as they found it expounded in Montesquieu, followed it with genuine scientific enthusiasm. The admirable expositions of the *Federalist* read like thoughtful applications of Montesquieu to the political needs and circumstances of America. They are full of the theory of checks and balances. The President is balanced off against Congress, Congress against the President, and each against the courts. . . . Politics is turned into mechanics under [Montesquieu's] touch. The theory of gravitation is supreme."[7]

But, according to Wilson, the "static" universe of Newtonian "balances and checks" had been superseded by the doctrine of scientific progress, a doctrine that views politics as a "living organism."

> [G]overnment is not a machine, but a living thing. It falls, not under the theory of the universe, but under the theory of organic life. It is accountable to Darwin, not

to Newton. It is modified by its environment, necessitated by its tasks, shaped to its functions by the sheer pressure of life. No living thing can have its organs offset against each other as checks, and live. On the contrary, its life is dependent upon their quick cooperation, their ready response to the commands of instinct or intelligence, their amicable community of purpose. Living political constitutions must be Darwinian in structure and in practice.[8]

Thus from the point of view of the "organic" theory of government, separation of powers is antithetical to "amicable community of purpose"—a living organism cannot be divided against itself. This Progressive critique of the Founding finds its most powerful expression today in the rhetoric of the "living Constitution."

As we saw in Chapter Three, the assertion that *The Federalist* applied Montesquieu's thought mechanically to the Constitution is at best dubious. The Framers thought less of Montesquieu than of adapting the separation of powers to an "unmixed" regime.[9] Furthermore, any attempt to maintain that the authors of *The Federalist* applied Newtonian mechanics to politics ignores the significance of *The Federalist's* discussion of ambition, honor, love of fame, noble minds, reputation, and manly spiritedness—to say nothing of its commitment to human freedom. There may be traces of Hume's political thought in *The Federalist*,[10] but there is no evidence whatsoever that its authors adhered to any theory of mechanistic psychology.[11] So far from believing that reason is the "slave of the passions,"[12] *The Federalist* argued that the principal purpose of republican or constitutional government was to insure that "the reason, alone, of the public . . . [would] control and regulate the government." And in due course, "[t]he passions ought to be controlled and regulated by the government."[13] No one who reads *The Federalist,* or for that matter the writings of the Founding period, can believe that the Framers were enamored of any deterministic theories of human behavior. They spoke too eloquently of liberty to have been seduced by any simplistic notions of a determined universe.

The Framers intended the regime they were creating to be—not indeed a "mechanical" regime—but a *political* regime in the fullest sense. Partisanship in support of constitutional government was to be the necessary and ordinary spring to politics. Citizens of the new democratic republic would ordinarily be partisans of constitutional government because they were partisans of liberty.[14] Their attachment to democratic forms would not be a matter of indifference. Indeed, their attachment would be inspired by the hope of political liberty, not just the survival of the political organism. Wilson, in contrast, was apparently unable to distinguish between democracy and socialism.[15]

The constitutional separation of powers was seen by the Framers as the principal institutional device for ensuring that reason would control and regulate the government. Under a system of separated powers, the legislature is "best adapted to deliberation and wisdom," whereas the executive provides the "energy," which is necessary to "good government."[16] Indeed, the separation of powers holds out the prospect that constitutional government can be "good government" as well as nontyrannical government. Separation insulates the legislature, allowing it to perform its deliberative functions. Legislative power is different "by nature" from executive power, the one culminating in general laws and the other in the particular execution of the general laws. The legislative function is to deliberate about the general or public good. Deliberation is hampered—indeed vitiated—by the admixture of particular considerations. On the other hand, execution would not be energetic if its primary purpose was deliberation. The separation of powers thus looks forward to the rule of law as the rule of reason both with respect to the making of legislation and to its execution.

Wilson and the Progressives did not refer to the "reason of the public," but of the "organic *will*" of society. For Wilson, the notion that political liberty could be grounded in the "laws of nature and nature's God" had been exposed by Darwinism to be hopelessly outmoded. "Liberty fixed in an unalterable law," Wilson wrote, "would be no liberty at all."[17] As one later-day epigone of Wilson expressed it, "no man who is as well abreast of modern science as the Fathers were of eighteenth-century science believes any longer in unchanging human nature."[18] The only principle of liberty that can be recognized within the Darwinian universe is the freedom to change or progress, a change or progress that has no particular end or purpose. But, as anyone can see, under this principle of freedom it is extremely difficult—nay, impossible—to distinguish between liberty and necessity. It may be, as one of Wilson's bolder contemporaries phrased it, simply that every living organism—including the political community—is moved by "will to power," and that liberty is simply the extent to which organisms can "discharge their strength."

From Wilson's point of view, the fundamental distinction of constitutional government was not between legislative and executive power, but between politics and administration. "Administration," Wilson wrote, "lies outside the proper sphere of *politics*. Administrative questions are not political questions."[19] It was this distinction that Wilson believed would provide the theoretical ground for the construction of the administrative state. The state was the universal (and therefore rational) embodiment of the will of the people. The American Framers, on the other hand, sought to embody the *reason* of the people in constitutional majorities, and the separation of powers was integral to the representation of such majorities. John Marini writes that the idea of the positive state, which had its origins in the thought of Hegel, was alien to the Founders of the American Constitution: "The notion that the antinomy between state and society, individual and community, reason and will, could be resolved is mere 'utopian speculation,' for both federalists and anti-federalists alike."[20] Hence, the separation of powers was necessary to the idea of limited or constitutional government, a form of government that—unlike the positive state—

reserved some sphere of activities for the individual in the form of rights and liberties. The Constitution of 1787 was designed, above all, to be the guarantor of individual rights through the rule of law.

The advent of the administrative state, however, requires either the abolition or the radical reform of the Framers' idea of limited government. Once the administrative state is seen as the "rational" embodiment of the will of the people, there is no need to impose limits on either the power of government or the power of administration. A perfect coincidence of will and reason in the state makes any limitations on government unnecessary. Limits are necessitated by the defect of rationality (in *The Federalist's* phrase "the fallibility of human reason"), not its perfection. As Marini cogently notes,

> [i]n Wilson's view, the realm of politics is concerned with executive articulation of the national will and legislative embodiment of that will. Politics or government is the domain of will embodied in law, and administration is the non-political implementation of that will . . . The progressive view denied any limitation, in principle, of the power of the state precisely because it is the embodiment of the will of the people.[21]

The general will of the people must be translated into practice by administration. Whereas the articulation of the national will is political, the administration of that will must be nonpolitical. In short, it requires scientific administration; even though administration is necessarily particular, scientific administrators can become a universal class of bureaucrats who serve as the eidetic bridge, so to speak, between the general and the particular. As a universal class, enlightened bureaucrats will have the capacity to subordinate their private interests to the welfare of the nation as a whole—to the general or organic will of the nation.[22] As the nonpolitical executors of politically determined public policy, these technocrats will be immune from the ordinary human passions that are the stock and trade of political life.

It is thus the separation of politics and administration—not the separation of the three branches of government—that will form the basis of the administrative state. It represents the most advanced attempt to reconcile or overcome the tension between individual and community, as the general will of the people will be administered by a "universal" class of scientific administrators. Such a universal (reasoning) class would need no checks upon its scientific (nonpolitical) administration. As Wilson wrote, "[d]irectly exercised, in the oversight of the daily details and in the choice of the daily means of government, public criticism is of course a clumsy nuisance, a rustic handling delicate machinery."[23]

Separation of powers was seen by the Framers as a powerful means of insuring that lawmaking and execution would contain at least the potential for reasonableness. But in the Progressives' view, the theory of the organic state was itself a guarantee of reason. The general will of the people is rational because it becomes universalized in the positive state. No particular interests can be represented in this universal will, and since the people's will is rational by virtue of its universality, it is unnecessary to contrive further checks that might prove to be an obstacle to enlightened, rational administration. Limited government must therefore give way to unlimited or positive government, the principal object of which is to provide for the welfare of the whole, not to protect the rights of individuals.

Wilson, of course, was an advocate of the parliamentary form of government. Such wholesale reform of the Constitution, however, was beyond even the wildest dreams of the Progressives. Rather, reformers have concentrated on undermining the separation of powers in more limited (and more subtle) ways. Richard Neustadt represents the academically orthodox position when he writes that "[t]he constitutional convention of 1787 is supposed to have created a government of 'separated powers.' It did nothing of the sort. Rather, it created a government of separated institutions *sharing* powers."[24] Louis Fisher, a follower of Neustadt and an unabashed advocate of congressional supremacy, writes that "[t]he Constitution, for both theoretical and practical reasons, anticipates a government of powers that are largely shared but sometimes exclusive."[25] This view of the separation of powers leads Fisher, remarkably, to advocate "[t]he right of Congress to intervene in administration," and to lament that this intervention is "still being resisted."[26]

Even more remarkable, perhaps, is the fact that the Supreme Court has in most recent years—albeit by fits and starts—adopted the academic view. In *Buckley v. Valeo* (1976), for example, the Court in its *per curiam* decision stated that it is

> clear from the provisions of the Constitution itself, and from the Federalist Papers, that the Constitution by no means contemplates total separation of each of [the] three essential branches of Government. The President is a participant in the law-making process by virtue of his authority to veto bills enacted by Congress. The Senate is a participant in the appointive process by virtue of its authority to refuse to confirm persons nominated to office by the President. The men who met in Philadelphia in the summer of 1787 were practical statesmen, experienced in politics, who viewed the principle of separation of powers as a vital check against tyranny. But they likewise saw that a hermetic sealing off of the three branches of Government from one another would preclude the establishment of a Nation capable of governing itself effectively.[27]

The Court here, unlike the Framers in Philadelphia, saw no tension between the requirements of effective government and the requirements of nontyrannical government. If efficiency had been the main object of the Framers, it is unlikely that they would have manifested such a concern for the separation of powers. They certainly knew that a monarchical form of government was administratively more "efficient" than a constitutional democracy. Yet, in their quaintness, they seem to have been more attached to liberty than to administrative efficiency.

But, of course, the Framers of the Constitution knew "that the true test of a good government is its aptitude and tendency to produce a good administration."[28] Good administration in a constitutional democracy depends on the separation of powers insofar as it allows for "energetic" execution. "A feeble executive," Hamilton wrote, "implies a feeble execution of the government. A feeble execution is but another phrase for a bad execution; and a government ill executed, whatever it may be in theory, must be, in practice, a bad government."[29] Administration by the legislative branch would provide a feeble execution in precisely the sense Hamilton is talking about. "The administration of government," Hamilton cautioned, "falls peculiarly within the province of the executive department."[30] The unity, dispatch, secrecy, and energy that are necessary to efficient administration belong to the executive. Hamilton, in a statement he knew to belabor the obvious, wrote that "decision, *secrecy,* and dispatch, are incompatible with the genius of a body so variable and so numerous" as the Congress.[31]

Good government requires that administration be the exclusive province of the executive. But, as the Framers well knew, the legislature would continually attempt to invade this executive province. Robert Dixon, an acute observer of legislative–executive relations, notes that "Congress has an instinctive thrust toward control of the executive. It seeks ever-greater authority over executive personnel and pursues a variety of other devices toward shared administration."[32] Indeed, as Madison forcefully noted, the tendency of the legislative department is to extend "the sphere of its activity" and draw "all power into its impetuous vortex."[33] This has certainly been the thrust of legislative activity throughout American history, but, as we will see, it is critically evident today. As Dixon remarks, "[t]he history of legislative-executive relationships has been marked by a steady pressure from Congress to adopt measures and procedures conceptually closer to a regime of shared powers than to the separation the framers envisioned."[34]

The Framers certainly understood that if the executive was to serve as the principal architect of sound administration, then the office must be fortified by the separation of powers and checks and balances. Madison only seems to be speaking paradoxically when he notes that in order to maintain the separation of powers in practice it is necessary first to mix and blend the powers. This is the principal thrust of the separation of powers—to create an *independent* executive.

It is true that the system of checks and balances provides some intermingling and interblending of the powers of government. But it is not to be inferred from this that the Framers intended a regime of "shared administration." Rather, as seen in Chapter Three, the purpose was a practical one. Without the defensive mechanisms of checks and balances, the separation of powers in a popular regime would, in practice, be reduced to mere "parchment barriers." Without some interblending of the various powers of government, there could be no separation of powers in practice. Thus, the emphatic purpose of the blending is to reinforce the separation of powers. In the *Federalist,* Hamilton responded to "objections" that the Constitution "confounds . . . authorities in the same body in violation of that important and well-established maxim which requires a separation between the different departments of power." Hamilton not only denied any violation of the "well-established maxim" but argued that some intermixture of powers was necessary to the maxim. "This partial intermixture is even, in some cases, not only proper but necessary to the mutual defense of the several members of the government against each other."[35]

It was not too many years ago that the Supreme Court understood this crucial feature of the separation of powers. Justice George Sutherland, writing for the Court in *O'Donoghue v. U.S.* (1933), stated that

> [t]he Constitution, in distributing the powers of government, creates three distinct and separate departments—the legislative, the executive, and the judicial. This separation is not merely a matter of convenience or of governmental mechanism. Its object is basic and vital . . . namely, to preclude a commingling of these essentially different powers of government in the same hands. And this object is none the less apparent and controlling because there is to be found in the Constitution an occasional specific provision conferring upon a given department certain functions, which, by their nature, would otherwise fall within the general scope of the powers of another. Such exceptions serve rather to emphasize the generally inviolate character of the plan.[36]

Today, however, the Supreme Court and respectable academic commentators interpret the constitutional checks and balances, not as defensive mechanisms allowing the different branches to maintain their independence, but as an indication that the Framers contemplated some form of "shared administration." Thus the court has held that as long as the "core functions" of the executive—those "central to the functioning of the Executive Branch"—remain inviolate, the legislature can share or authorize the courts to share power that otherwise would be within the exclusive province of the executive.

The Supreme Court, however, remains the sole determiner of the functions that are central to the executive branch. And, although the Court has been exceptionally jealous of any attempts to encroach upon its own prerogatives,[37] it has been more than willing to cooperate with the Congress in its forays upon executive power. In a statement rendered almost incomprehensible by its naiveté, Chief Justice Rehnquist remarked in the *Morrison* case that Congress's creation of the office of special prosecutor in the Ethics in Government Act did "not involve an attempt by Congress to increase its own powers at the expense of the Executive Branch."[38] The act had purportedly increased judicial power relative to that of the executive and it was this fact, presumably, that led

Rehnquist to consider the congressional action as self-effacing. But as amazing as it might appear at first glance, Rehnquist does not seem to realize the basic fact that in the American constitutional system every diminution of executive power is simultaneously an augmentation of legislative power.

For the past twenty-five years or more, Congress has become less interested in deliberating on general questions of public policy (the role envisioned by the Framers) and more interested in controlling the details of executive administration. Congress prefers to leave the difficult questions of public policy to be decided by the executive or judicial branch. It would much rather leave such controversial questions as abortion and affirmative action to the judicial branch to decide. One of the many curious features of the ill-fated confirmation hearings of Judge Robert Bork was the fact that Bork insisted that steps must be taken to restore the separation of powers by curbing the judicial activism of the courts and deferring policy decisions to the Congress. Ordinarily, one would suppose that the members of the Senate Judiciary Committee who were considering Bork's nomination would have been delighted to hear such support for Congress's policy role. The Senate's reaction, however, was unequivocal. No Senator (or House member) wants the Congress to resume its primary role in the formulation of public policy. Congress prefers to defer the difficult and politically risky legislative decisions to the courts and the executive branch.

The reason is not difficult to fathom. Congress has discovered that the most certain route to incumbency is not in deliberating about the national interest, but in providing constituency services in the executive bureaucracy. As Morris Fiorina has stated, members of Congress "are increasingly deemphasizing their role as formulators of national policies—a controversial role, after all—and emphasizing their role as ombudsmen who strike fear into the hearts of incompetent or arbitrary bureaucrats."[39] Typically, Congress passes general legislation containing vague and non-controversial goals (e.g., clean air, clean water, full employment, fair competition, etc.). It is left to the administrative agencies to fill in the details and to provide the rules and regulations. Real decisions on the part of the Congress are certain to antagonize powerful interest groups that are affected by the legislation. As Fiorina describes it,

> Why take political chances by setting detailed regulations sure to antagonize some political actor or another? Why not require an agency to do the dirty work and then step in to redress the grievances that result from its activities? Let the agency take the blame and the member of Congress the credit. In the end everybody benefits. Members successfully wage their campaigns for re-election. And while popularly vilified, bureaucrats get their rewards in the committee rooms of Congress.[40]

The symbiotic relationship that exists between Congress and the bureaucracy makes it virtually impossible for the president to control the bureaucracy. The unelected bureaucrats are only too willing to bear the brunt of public wrath in return for increased funding that allows them to magnify their functions and increase their numbers. At the same time, the increase of the reach of the executive bureaucracy into the ordinary lives of citizens increases the individual Congressmember's role as ombudsman. Thus both the Congress and the bureaucracy profit from acting on the strongest imperative of the administrative state—that "the unregulated life is not worth living."

Congress has developed a number of institutional devices, some called "nonstatutory controls,"[41] to increase its influence over the executive branch. Most important have been the congressional reforms aimed at the decentralization of its own power structure. Decentralization has increased the power of individual committee and subcommittee chairmen (and their staffs) over the executive agencies they are charged to oversee. As Fiorina rightly notes,

> the Congress has had a standing committee system for more than 150 years, but the major trend of the twentieth century has been a decentralizing one. The party leadership lost power to the committee leadership, which in turn lost power to the subcommittee leadership. All of this has occurred under the guise of democratic 'reforms' to be sure. But we should not forget that the impact has been one of ever-increasing division of the power to control the bureaucracy.[42]

The upshot of decentralization within Congress has been that "[m]embers of Congress are given the opportunity to exercise disproportionate influence over segments of the federal bureaucracy that are of special concern to them."[43] Perhaps the most unsettling aspect of this development is the extent to which decentralization has also increased the access of special interests to congressional committees and the extent to which it has become easier for special interests to influence policy decisions. Typically, congressional staff will serve as interest brokers between special interest groups and the relevant executive agencies targeted by an interest group. Thus the representative functions of Congress have been almost completely replaced by special interest brokering—hardly the representative democracy that the Framers envisioned!

Congress is rendered impotent as an instrument of national policy by decentralization. As one congressional scholar has aptly remarked, "the resulting dispersion of power within Congress, and the refusal to allow strong centralized leadership, ensures that congressional decisions on major policy matters (unless aided and pushed by an outside leader) will be incremental at best, immobilized and incoherent as a norm."[44] More importantly, under these circumstances it is impossible to hold Congress accountable for its failure to deliberate on issues of national interest. Members of Congress who provide efficient constituency services can assure electoral support "independent of policy or ideological considerations."[45] The people never have a chance in the electoral scheme to judge Congress as an institution, only its individual members.

Numerous opinion polls indicate that Congress is held in very low esteem by the American people. It is clear that, as an institution, Congress is much more liberal than the people. The fact that national majorities have elected

"conservatives" in five of the last six presidential elections is only one indication of this fact. The Democratic party seems almost to have abandoned any
serious attempt to contest presidential elections, apparently content to dominate
the legislature. If Congress can continue to consolidate its power over the executive bureaucracy, then it will be able to administer the government without
having to take electoral responsibility. The president will thus have the responsibility for administration without the power to control the administrative bureaucracy. It is little wonder that the Democrats seem to be more than willing to
leave the presidency to the Republicans. Of course, the fact that Congress and
the president represent different majorities, as noted in Chapter Three, is the
necessary condition for an effective separation of powers. But it is when Congress, using a variety of guises and deceptions politely termed "nonstatutory
controls," tries to interfere in the details of execution that serious problems
involving the separation of powers arise. The main problem is that Congress's
interference in the details of executive administration makes it impossible for
the president to perform his constitutional duty to "take Care that the Laws be
faithfully executed" (Art. II, §3). The Constitution not only gives the president
the responsibility, but the sole power to execute the law. This unification of
power and responsibility is, of course, a necessary condition of constitutional
government and is the principal object of the separation of powers. The ultimate
end of separating the powers of government is to make possible the rule of law
and thus the protection of individual liberties.

Over the years, Congress has perfected its "nonstatutory controls" over
administration. The personal power of committee and subcommittee chairmen
is the most important of these controls. Budget language, instructions in committee reports, investigations, threats of investigation and prosecution, threats
to reduce appropriations, and threats to abolish the jobs of recalcitrant bureaucrats are just a few of the means used by members of Congress to control or
influence executive administration. In the appropriations bill authorizing fiscal
1990 funding for the Department of Interior, for example, a provision was
inserted that made it illegal for Interior employees to make any record or report
(either orally or in writing) any contacts with members of Congress or their
staff to the secretary of the Interior. Mark Leidel comments that "Such Orwell-
ian tactics might make Mikhail Gorbachev shudder, but they are becoming
business as usual in a Washington increasingly divided by a constitutional
power struggle between the executive and legislative branches of government."[46] In the face of vigorous protests from the executive branch, Congress
withdrew the offending clause, but only after it had been in effect for one day,
thus setting a precedent for similar intrusions in the future. It is a rare
bureaucrat—whether a political appointee or career civil servant—who can
withstand the determined imprecations of a committee or subcommittee chair
(or their staff).[47] Members of Congress know that their ability to control administration is the key to their own electoral fortunes. Therefore the stakes are

high. At the same time, the subtle insinuation of the legislative branch into executive affairs blurs lines of responsibility and therefore renders accountability of both Congress and the executive difficult, if not impossible. The fact that voters are pleased with individual members of Congress conceals in great measure the extent to which Congress as a whole has made dangerous inroads upon executive power. As Madison presciently remarked in *The Federalist,* "the constitutional powers [of the legislature] being at once more extensive, and less susceptible of precise limits, it can, with the greater facility, make under complicated and indirect measures, the encroachments which it makes on the co-ordinate departments."[48] The "complicated and indirect measures" will probably never result in a sudden or dramatic usurpation of power by the legislature, but will tend towards a "gradual concentration" of power.[49] Indeed, the concentration of power will hardly be noticed, especially if it is justified in terms of increasing the efficiency of government or the necessity of extending the reach of the administrative state in order to serve the welfare of the people.

But Congress has made open statutory forays against executive power as well. The Supreme Court has approved some and disallowed others without delineating a settled principle by which the conflicting claims of the executive and legislative branches can be adjudicated. Although it is difficult to discern a consistent line of reasoning in the cases, the most recent decisions seem to indicate that the Court is in the process of adopting the "shared administration" view of the separation of powers. Among the several statutory devices the Congress has created, the most successful have been the legislative veto and prosecution under the Ethics in Government Act.

Although declared unconstitutional in *I.N.S. v. Chadha* (1983), congressional use of the legislative veto has continued unabated. As Louis Fisher notes, between 1983 and 1986 alone Congress passed 103 new bills containing legislative veto provisions. "The new legislative vetoes are more offensive than the one-house veto struck down by the Supreme Court in *Chadha.* They are usually vetoes given to the Appropriations committees."[50] All were signed by President Reagan, although he did register complaints on occasion that the provisions were unconstitutional and that the executive was therefore not bound by them. Fisher's analysis of the *Chadha* decision reeks of high dungeon: "the Supreme Court adopted a highly formalistic model of the relationship between Congress and the President. The net effect is to instruct Congress that it has no business in executive affairs. Predictably, Congress has ignored the Court's preaching, as it should."[51]

Included in legislation, the legislative veto allows Congress (one or both houses), a committee, or a subcommittee to veto executive branch activities without the concurrence of the president. In effect, it reserves to Congress the right to interfere in the details of executive administration by vetoing or threatening to veto actions of executive agencies or of the president. At issue in the *Chadha* case was the provision of the Immigration and Naturalization Act that allowed either house of Congress to veto the attorney general's decision to suspend proceedings against otherwise deportable aliens when the deportation would cause "an extreme hardship." Congress had delegated this power to the executive branch to rid itself of the onerous task of having to pass private bills for each individual who was to be exempted from deportation. As provided by the act, the attorney general transmitted a report of suspensions to Congress, which included the name of Chadha and 339 others. The House of Representatives exercised its one house veto option, passing a resolution opposing the suspension of deportation proceedings against Chadha and five others. The reason for Chadha's rejection has never been revealed. Because Congress has exempted itself from freedom of information laws, it is unlikely that the reason will ever be known.[52]

The Ninth Circuit Court of Appeals held that the legislative veto provision of the Immigration and Naturalization Act violated the separation of powers because it allowed the Congress to encroach upon "powers that are central or essential" to the operation of both the executive and judicial branches.[53] As a result of the legislative veto, the Court of Appeals maintained that "Aliens are no longer guaranteed the constraints of articulated reasons and stare decisis in the interpretation of the Immigration and Naturalization Act. Adjudications they have obtained in the Judicial branch may be set aside for any reason, or no reason at all, so that judicial decisions may be for naught." The court went on to note that

> there are virtually no procedural constraints on the ultimate congressional decision nor any provision for review of Congress' legal or factual conclusions . . . The legislature thus disrupts the judicial system by retaining a selective power to override individual adjudications, in lieu of changing standards prospectively by the usual, corrective device of a statutory amendment.[54]

As the court's discussion of executive power made clear, the fundamental constitutional defect of the legislative veto was the extent to which it allowed Congress to dictate the disposition of *individual* cases, or the extent to which it allowed Congress to descend from the general to the particular.

There is no doubt that Congress could have disposed of Chadha by passing a private bill. But once it delegated the responsibility to the executive branch, it could no longer determine or dictate the execution of the law with respect to individuals. Noting that the essential function of the executive under the Immigration and Naturalization Act was one of "law enforcement," the court reasoned that in the case of the legislative veto "there is interference with essential executive functions because the Executive's decision that the House reversed was reached after the Executive had given consideration to an individual case."[55] And this authority was "exercisable only in relation to the rights of a particular person under a legal standard subject to judicial interpretation and control for abuse."[56] Noting that whereas the Constitution authorizes Congress "to make all laws," the court nevertheless concluded that this could not be construed to grant Congress the prerogative "to exercise power in any way it deems convenient."[57]

Interestingly, the court of appeals did not consider the unicameral character of the legislative veto, nor the fact that it did not require presidential approval to be of decisive importance. The Supreme Court, however, ruled on precisely these grounds. Chief Justice Burger, writing for the majority, noted that "the fact that a given law or procedure is efficient, convenient, and useful in facilitating functions of government, standing alone, will not save it if it is contrary to the Constitution. Convenience and efficiency are not the primary objectives—or the hallmarks—of democratic government and our inquiry is sharpened rather than blunted by the fact that congressional veto provisions are appearing with increasing frequency in statutes that delegate authority to executive and independent agencies."[58] The chief justice pointed out that Article I procedural requirements are "explicit and unambiguous." Since the action of the House in invoking the legislative veto "was essentially legislative in purpose and effect,"[59] it must conform to the strict procedural requirements of Article I. It must pass both houses of Congress and be presented to the president for his approval.

Burger's proof of the legislative character of the veto is somewhat transparent, however. Absent the legislative veto provision in the act, Congress could not force the attorney general to deport an alien. The only way such action could be taken is for Congress to pass a private bill mandating the deportation.[60] But Chadha in this instance would be protected by the separation of powers in the sense that the bill would have to pass both houses of Congress, be signed by the president, and be subject to judicial scrutiny. Thus in Burger's reasoning, the legislative veto, insofar as it provides (in effect) a substitute for such legislation, is itself legislative in character. It makes more sense, however, to consider, as the court of appeals did, the legislative veto as an attempt to exercise executive or judicial power. The legislative veto in this instance was clearly an example of Congress attempting to apply the law in particular instances, i.e., to execute the law, and thereby obviate whatever judicial checks exist against the misuse of executive power. Whatever merit Burger's procedural argument might have, it fails to strike at the heart of the matter—the separation of powers is violated when Congress executes the law.

Justice Powell in his concurring opinion noted that "the House did not enact a general rule; rather it made its own determination that six specific persons did not comply with certain statutory criteria. It thus undertook the type of decision that traditionally has been left to other branches." Powell asserted that the House action was "clearly adjudicatory."[61] It would seem, however, that the House's action was executive rather than adjudicatory, but the point is still the same: the attempt to apply a general rule to specific persons was the gravamen of the action that violated the separation of powers. And in

Chadha's case, the action of the House (in the absence of any challenge to the legislative veto provision itself) foreclosed the possibility of a check against the abuse of Chadha's individual rights. The Congress may have acted in a purely arbitrary and capricious manner. Because the legislative veto decision was not subject to any separation of powers checks, the rights of one individual were exposed to the decision of the House (in reality to the decision of the staff of a committee), a decision that it did not have to justify or explain but only had to announce. This is hardly what the Framers had in mind when they envisioned the separation of powers as the bulwark of the rule of law and individual liberties. Although the legislative veto provision contained in the Immigration and Nationality Act was somewhat unusual in that its exercise directly affected the rights of individuals, all legislative veto provisions are, in one way or another, attempts to control the particular details of execution and are therefore just as questionable from the point of view of the separation of powers.

Justice Byron White wrote a frantic dissent, arguing that the legislative veto was an "indispensable political invention"[62] of "the modern administrative state."[63] The advent of the modern administrative state has necessitated, White argued, the delegation of legislative authority to the executive and to independent regulatory agencies. Massive delegation appears to be the imperative of the administrative state; therefore devices such as the legislative veto are necessary to control or supervise delegated power. White thus appears to agree with those who argue that the Framers' view of the separation of powers has been superseded by the "deep structure of the Constitution's evolving grammar," an evolving grammar that is said to have ratified the administrative state just as surely as if the Constitution had been amended by regular constitutional procedures.[64]

White poses this logical postulate: "If Congress may delegate lawmaking power to independent and Executive agencies, it is most difficult to understand Art I as prohibiting Congress from also reserving a check on legislative power for itself."[65] It is beyond cavil that Congress can reserve to itself means to check delegated power, but it cannot, consistent with the Congress, do so by abrogating to itself executive or judicial functions. It must do so by legislative means and, Burger's opinion to the contrary notwithstanding, the exercise of the legislative veto under the Immigration Act was an attempt to execute the law, not an exercise in lawmaking or legislative oversight. As such, the legislative veto is clearly a violation of the separation of powers, and in the case of Chadha pointed dramatically to the close connection between the constitutional structure of separated powers and the protection of individual liberties. Madison was not exaggerating when he described the separation of powers as "an essential precaution in favor of liberty."[66]

In *Bowsher v. Synar* (1986), the Supreme Court reaffirmed the *Chadha* decision by noting that "once Congress makes its choice in enacting legislation, its participation ends. Congress can thereafter control the execution of its enactment only indirectly—by passing new legislation."[67] At issue in *Bowsher* was the constitutionality of the provision of the Gramm-Rudman-Hollings Act, which gave power to the comptroller general to determine when sequestration orders mandating spending reductions must be issued by the president. The Court found that the duties of the comptroller general under the act were executive in nature: "Interpreting a law enacted by Congress to implement the legislative mandate is the very essence of 'execution' of the law . . . the Comptroller General must exercise judgment concerning facts that affect the application of the Act."[68]

The comptroller general is nominated to the office by the president from a list of three individuals recommended by the Speaker of the House and the president pro tempore of the Senate and is confirmed by the Senate. The comptroller general is removable, however, only by Congress, either by impeachment or by joint resolution for specified causes, among them "inefficiency," "neglect of duty," and "malfeasance." As these terms imply, the tenure of the comptroller general rests, in reality, solely on the will of Congress. Going on the commonsense principle that "once an officer is appointed, it is only the authority that can remove him, and not the authority that appointed him, that he must fear and, in the performance of his functions, obey," the Court concluded that since "the structure of the Constitution does not permit Congress to execute the laws, it follows that Congress cannot grant to an officer under its control what it does not possess."[69] The execution of the laws by an officer controlled by Congress "would be, in essence, to permit a congressional veto. Congress could simply remove, or threaten to remove, an officer for executing the laws in any fashion found to be unsatisfactory to Congress."[70] Congress, the Court reiterated, is not permitted by the principle of separation of powers to execute the laws, either directly or indirectly.

As the Court made clear in *Buckley v. Valeo* (1976), Art. II, cl. 2 of the Constitution, while allowing the Congress to vest the appointment of inferior officers "as they think proper, in the President alone, in the Courts of Law, or in the Heads of Departments," necessarily precludes appointment by Congress. Even without the constitutional proscription, a just inference from the separation of powers would prevent the Congress from appointing officers who exercised executive duties. But what about executive officers appointed by the judiciary? This was the question posed in *Morrison v. Olson* (1988).

Rebuffed in its attempts to appoint executive officers in *Buckley,* Congress decided in passing the Ethics in Government Act in 1978 to rely on the courts for the appointment of special prosecutors. What appeared to Chief Justice Rehnquist and other members of the Supreme Court as a self-effacing act was in fact a conscious and determined act of self-aggrandizement on the apart of Congress. The fact that the Ethics in Government Act applies only to the executive branch and not to Congress should be a clue to anyone with eyes to see that Congress intended to use this law as a weapon against the executive, at the same time insuring that the powerful office of the special prosecutor could never be used against the Congress itself. Congress has in recent years regularly exempted itself from legislation. In addition to the Ethics in Government Act, Congress has exempted itself from coverage under the Freedom of Information Act, the Civil Rights Restoration Act of 1988, the Age Discrimination Act, the Privacy Act, and a host of others. Yet, in *The Federalist*, Madison touted the fact that under the new Constitution members of Congress could "make no law which will not have its full operation on themselves" as one of the most powerful republican checks against tyranny. If the "vigilant and manly spirit which actuates the people of America," Madison wrote, "should ever be so far debased as to tolerate a law not obligatory on the legislature, as well as on the people, the people will be prepared to tolerate anything but liberty."[71] These are indeed strong words, but Madison was certainly not one to underestimate the potential for legislative tyranny.

One of the most disturbing recent trends in contemporary American politics is the use of criminal prosecution for political purposes, a practice redolent of the last days of the Roman Republic. No one can fail to see that the *Morrison* case was fueled by fierce political partisanship. But when partisanship is coupled with prosecution or the threat of prosecution, the rule of law becomes simply an ill-disguised charade.

In *Morrison* the issue was the constitutionality of judicial appointment of an executive officer. The Ethics in Government Act, passed in 1978, was described by Judge Ruth Bader Ginsburg, in her dissent in the Court of Appeals, as a "response to the Watergate era abuses of the executive branch, abuses which themselves threatened the balance between the three branches of government."[72] However much hyperbole this statement indulges, the Ethics in Government Act was clearly an attempt to debilitate the executive branch.

As Judge Silberman, writing for the majority, remarked, the Act "violate[s] the Constitution because it impermissibly interferes with the President's constitutional duty to 'take Care that the Laws be faithfully executed'."[73] The "[a]uthority to prosecute an individual," Silberman continued, is that government power which most threatens personal liberty, for a prosecutor "has the power to employ the full machinery of the state in scrutinizing any given individual. Even if a defendant is ultimately acquitted, forced immersion in criminal investigation and adjudication is a wrenching disruption of everyday life'."[74] Thus separation of powers is designed, in great measure, to protect individuals from abuse of governmental discretion. A special prosecutor who is not responsible to the president and can proceed on different standards and rules than those adhered to by the Justice Department makes it impossible for the president to execute the laws uniformly and therefore "faithfully." Silberman rightly notes that "the Constitution vests the power to initiate a criminal prosecution exclusively in the Executive Branch."[75] Not only did the Constitution lodge prosecution in the executive branch because, by nature, it is an executive function, but also a unitary executive would fix responsibility for the exercise of this dangerous power. "The Framers provided for a unitary executive," Silberman writes, "to ensure that the branch wielding the power to enforce the law would be accountable to the people." Furthermore, Presidential accountability "is not merely an abstract idea of political theory," but the "hallmark of our democracy."[76] As Judge Silberman concluded,

> The Ethics in Government Act, it seems to us, deliberately departs from this framework in both its particular provisions and in its general purpose, which is to authorize an officer not accountable to any elected official to prosecute crimes. It may well be that the Constitutional framework is awkward or burdensome in particular cases, but, under this system, efficiency is knowingly sacrificed in various ways so that liberty may be protected.[77]

The court of appeals thus concluded that the act entrusts "a core executive" function to a special prosecutor not accountable to the president. This, Judge Silberman concluded, violated the fundamental principle of the separation of powers.

The Supreme Court, however, did not agree with Silberman's analysis, stating that "we do not think that appointment of the independent counsels by the court runs afoul of the constitutional limitation on 'incongruous' interbranch appointments."[78] Supervision of the special prosecutors's discretion was not judged to be "so central to the functioning of the Executive Branch as to require as a matter of constitutional law that the counsel be terminable at will by the President."[79]

Some history of the origins of the case is in order. The case arose out of a dispute between the president and Congress. Two subcommittees of the House in the course of conducting oversight hearings into the administration of the Superfund by the Environmental Protection Agency subpoenaed numerous internal EPA documents. The president responded by ordering the EPA administrator not to surrender the documents and by having the attorney general notify the committees that he was invoking executive privilege. Theodore Olson, who was assistant attorney general in the Office of Legal Counsel, advised the president in his decision to assert executive privilege. The House, in response, voted a contempt citation against the EPA administrator for failure to produce the requested documents. The district court declined to intervene, urging the parties to compromise their differences. Eventually the president and the House committees did reach an agreement giving the committee limited access to the documents under question.

The House Judiciary Committee began an investigation into the actions of the Justice Department—without the knowledge of the minority members of the committee—that lasted two and one-half years. Eventually the committee produced a report of more than 3,000 pages impugning the truthfulness of the testimony given by Olson before the committee during the investigation. This report was sent to the attorney general with a request that he seek the appointment of an independent counsel to investigate the report's allegations.[80] Under the Ethics in Government Act, the attorney general must apply for the appointment of an independent counsel within 90 days unless he finds "there are no reasonable grounds to believe that further investigation or prosecution is warranted." In conducting the investigation, however, the attorney general is prohibited from using routine investigatory techniques: "the Attorney General shall have no authority to convene grand juries, plea bargain, grant immunity, or issue subpoenas." Under these circumstances it is virtually impossible for the Attorney General to certify that "there are no reasonable grounds . . . for further investigation." In reply to the majority's strained attempt to maintain that the attorney general retained substantial discretion in whether or not to recommend the appointment of an independent counsel, Justice Scalia remarked, in his lone dissent, that "[a]s a practical matter, it would be surprising if the Attorney General had any choice . . . but to seek appointment of an independent counsel to pursue the charges against the principal object of the congressional request, Mr. Olson. Merely the political consequences (to him and to the president) of seeming to break the law by refusing to do so would have been substantial. How could it not be, the public would ask, that a 3,000-page indictment drawn by our representatives over 2½ years does not even establish 'reasonable grounds to believe' that further investigation or prosecution is warranted with respect to at least the principal alleged culprit?"[81] It is true, as the majority points out, that the attorney general's decision is not reviewable by any court. But as Scalia replies, since the attorney general must submit a report to the requesting committee in the event he decides not to seek an appointment, the "Congress is not prevented from reviewing it [and] the context of the statute is acrid with the smell of threatened impeachment."[82] As Scalia trenchantly points out, "by the application of this statute in the present case, Congress has effectively compelled a criminal investigation of a high-level appointee of the President in connection with his actions arising out of a bitter power dispute between the President and the Legislative Branch."[83]

For Chief Justice Rehnquist, writing for the 7–1 majority, the resolution of the case revolved around the constitutionality of the act's provision for appointments of independent counsel by a Special Division of the United States Court of Appeals for the District of Columbia Circuit. More particularly, the question was whether the interbranch appointment deprived the president of a core function of his office in violation of the separation of powers. The threshold question here was whether the independent counsel was an inferior officer in terms of the Constitution's appointment clause. Article II, Section 2 provides that the president shall appoint "all other Officers of the United States, whose Appointments are not herein otherwise provided for, and which shall be established by Law; but the Congress may by Law vest the Appointment of such inferior

Officers, as they think proper, in the President alone, in the Court of Law, or in the Heads of Departments." Thus Congress could only vest the appointment of the independent counsel in the courts if the office was an "inferior" one.

The chief justice enumerated four reasons as to why the independent counsel was "an 'inferior' officer in the constitutional sense."[84] First is the fact that the independent counsel "is subject to removal by a higher Executive Branch official." The chief justice did, however, note some qualifications: "Although [the independent counsel] may not be 'subordinate' to the Attorney General (and the President) insofar as she possesses a degree of independent discretion to exercise the powers delegated to her under the Act, the fact that she can be removed by the Attorney General indicates that she is *to some degree* 'inferior' in rank and authority."[85] The independent counsel can be removed by the attorney general "only for good cause, physical disability, mental incapacity, or any other condition that substantially impairs the performance of such independent counsel's duties."[86] Upon removal, the attorney general must submit in writing "a report specifying the facts found and the ultimate grounds for such removal" to the Special Division and to both judiciary committees. The committees, at their discretion, can make the report public.[87] In addition, the independent counsel can contest the removal by obtaining "judicial review of the removal in a civil action" in the U.S. District Court for the District of Columbia.[88] Thus it is more than a bit misleading to contend that the independent counsel is "removable by a higher Executive Branch official." Given the fact that the attorney general is removable at the sole discretion of the president might cast some doubt on Rehnquist's rather facile identification of the independent counsel as an "inferior" office in the constitutional sense of the term.

The second factor in Rehnquist's decision was that the independent counsel "is empowered by the Act to perform only certain, limited duties. An independent counsel's role is restricted primarily to investigation and, if appropriate, prosecution for certain federal crimes."[89] Again, Rehnquist finds it necessary to qualify his statement: "Admittedly the Act delegates to [the independent counsel] 'full power and independent authority to exercise all investigative and prosecutorial functions and powers of the Department of Justice.'"[90] But, again, the chief justice understates this colossal exception. In fact, the independent counsel has *more* power to pursue investigative and prosecutorial functions than the attorney general does! The independent counsel is given the power of "contesting in court . . . any claim of privilege or attempt to withhold evidence on grounds of national security."[91] This is a power *not* given to the attorney general. In addition, according to the act, "an independent counsel shall, *except where not possible,* comply with the written or other established policies of the Department of Justice respecting enforcement of the criminal laws."[92] This is particularly important with respect to the evidentiary requirements for prosecution. Justice Department regulations require that an indictment issue only if the prosecutor has reason to believe that an unbiased jury would convict. Lawrence

Walsh, independent counsel in the Iran-Contra case, has stated that he would seek indictments whenever there was probable cause to believe that a crime has been committed.[93] This situation, of course, makes it impossible for the president to execute the laws faithfully. Whatever else "faithfully" might mean, it certainly means that the same standards of prosecution must be applied to all individuals. Changing standards of prosecution undermines any possibility of the rule of law.[94]

The third factor was the fact that the independent counsel's office "is limited in jurisdiction."[95] It is true that the reach of the independent counsel's power extends only to specified executive branch officials—Congress is exempted from the coverage of the act. The independent counsel must also act within the scope of the jurisdiction granted by the special division. The attorney general may request an expansion of the prosecutorial jurisdiction of the independent counsel, but may not request that it be contracted. In practice, however, the Special Division has interpreted the jurisdiction of the independent counsel quite broadly. The attorney general had initially refused to ask for a special prosecutor for two of Olson's Department of Justice colleagues. Independent counsel Morrison asked the attorney general to request expanded jurisdiction from the Special Division. When he refused, saying there was no reason for further investigation in their case, Morrison requested the Special Division to expand the jurisdiction. The Special Division quite appropriately held that it was beyond its power to do so, but it did hold that the original jurisdiction to investigate Olson was broad enough to include investigations of the other two!

The final factor adduced by Chief Justice Rehnquist was the fact that the independent counsel's "office is limited in tenure." "There is, Rehnquist writes, "concededly no time limit on the appointment of a particular counsel."[96] Indeed, by law the tenure of the independent counsel is, for all intents and purposes, self-determined. It is up to the independent counsel to determine when "the investigation of all matters within the prosecutorial jurisdiction . . . has been completed or . . . substantially completed." It is true that the Special Division can terminate an independent counsel on its own motion or at the request of the attorney general, but in practice it is most likely that the determination will rest with the independent counsel. All of this amounts to a determination in the opinion of eight members of the Court that the independent counsel is an "inferior officer" for purposes of the appointments clause. This, despite the fact that the independent counsel has more power and discretion in some instances than the attorney general, admittedly not an "inferior officer", and is more difficult to remove from office than any member of the president's cabinet.

Even with the determination that the independent counsel is an "inferior officer," the question remained as to whether interbranch appointments are allowable under the appointments clause. As the chief justice remarks, "[o]n its face" the appointments clause "admits of no limitation on interbranch appointments. Indeed, the inclusion of 'as they think proper' seems clearly to give Congress significant discretion to determine whether it is 'proper' to vest the appointment of, for example, executive officials in the 'courts of Law'."[97] Obviously the appointment of inferior officers in the same branch was the principal thrust of this exception to the appointments clause. In this instance there would be no separation of powers considerations. The Court approved (*Ex Parte Siebold* [1880]) an interbranch appointment where Congress authorized judges to appoint election supervisors. Here the courts were appointing legislative officers who were performing legislative duties and who were ultimately responsible to Congress. In the *Morrison* case, however, the Special Division appoints executive officers who perform executive duties and who report to Congress! The analogy is anything but apt.

Congressional oversight of the independent counsel is not merely theoretical or formal. The relevant congressional committees "have oversight jurisdiction with respect to the official conduct of any independent counsel" and can require "reports on the activities" of the independent counsel. Most ominously, however, is the requirement that "[a]n independent counsel shall advise the House of Representatives of any substantial and credible information which such independent counsel receives, in carrying out the independent counsel's responsibilities under this chapter that may constitute grounds for an impeachment."[98] This latter requirement (which Scalia had characterized as "acrid with the smell of threatened impeachment") insures that the independent counsel will be, in fact if not in theory, responsible to the Congress and not the president or the attorney general.

The issue of removability is also crucial to presidential responsibility. *Myers v. U.S.* (1926) had determined that an integral part of executive power was the power to remove executive officers without interference from Congress. *Humphrey's Executor* (1935) did place restrictions upon the president's power of removal for those officers who exercised "quasi-legislative" and "quasi-judicial" functions. Presumably the distinction between the two cases was that the president's power of removal (in the latter case for "good cause" only) could be limited to the extent that the officer exercised nonexecutive powers. But a purely executive officer should be responsible to the president alone. Rehnquist's reasoning in this respect was so forced as to strain all credulity. "We undoubtedly did rely on the terms 'quasi-legislative' and 'quasi-judicial,'" Rehnquist asserts, "to distinguish the officials involved in Humphrey's Executor . . . from those in Myers, but our present considered view is that the determination of whether the Constitution allows Congress to impose a 'good cause'-type restriction on the President's power to remove an official cannot be made to turn on whether or not that official is classified as 'purely executive.'"[99] The "real question" is not to fix executive responsibility, but to determine "whether the removal restrictions are of such a nature that they impede the President's ability to perform his constitutional duty, and the functions of the officials in question must be analyzed in that light."[100] But the chief justice easily reconciles himself to the fact that the constitutional functions are not impeded by the removal restrictions. There is no doubt that the independent counsel's functions are those that have "typically" been undertaken by executive branch officials. But since the independent counsel is "an inferior officer . . . with limited jurisdiction and tenure and lacking policymaking or significant administrative authority," the Court does not consider the limitations on the president's removal powers to contravene the Constitution.[101] Thus according to the chief justice, the only limitation on Congress's power to create interbranch appointments is "if such provisions for appointment had the potential to impair the constitutional functions assigned to one of the branches."[102] This would be the only occasion that would run "afoul of the constitutional limitation on 'incongruous' interbranch appointments."[103]

Justice Scalia's dissent was justly acerb. As he rightly pointed out, prosecution is not "typically" executive in nature but "a quintessentially executive function."[104] From Scalia's point of view "it is ultimately irrelevant *how much* the statute reduces presidential control. The case is over when the Court acknowledges, as it must, that '[i]t is undeniable that the Act reduces the amount of control or supervision that the Attorney General and, through him, the President exercises over the investigation and prosecution of a certain class of alleged criminal activity.' "[105] It is certainly true, as Scalia points out, that "the primary check against prosecutorial abuse is a political one."[106] It is the president, not the independent counsel, who is responsible to the people. But, if the independent counsel is ultimately responsible to Congress, then there can be no clear electoral responsibility for the actions of the independent counsel. Under these circumstances, Congress can indeed "mask, under complicated and indirect measures, the encroachments which it makes on the co-ordinate departments."[107] There can be little doubt that the independent counsel provision of the Ethics in Government Act is a powerful means by which Congress can evade public accountability. It does this by keeping effective control over the independent counsel for itself and parceling the responsibility for the faithful execution of the laws to the president. As one acute observer has recently remarked, "the independent counsel statute is both an example of [the] process for circumventing public accountability, and a means for preserving [the] process."[108]

Scalia also reminds us of something that we should never have forgotten: "The purpose of the separation and equilibrium of powers in general, and of the unitary Executive in particular, was not merely to assure effective government but to preserve individual freedom."[109] Individual freedom is guaranteed just as much to those who occupy executive offices as those who occupy seats in Congress. But executive officers can be prosecuted under different standards and Congress is exempt from the statute. Hardly the rule of law the Framers had in mind in fashioning the separation of powers. As Scalia remarks, "[t]his is not only not the government of laws that the Constitution established; it is not a government of laws at all."[110]

What is perhaps even more disturbing in the *Morrison* case is the collusion between two branches of the government to aggrandize their own power at the expense of the presidency. This is particularly egregious since (as seen in Chapter Three) it was settled long ago that "[d]eciding whether a matter has in any measure been committed by the Constitution to another branch of government, or whether the action of that branch exceeds whatever authority has been committed, is itself a delicate exercise in constitutional interpretation, and is a responsibility of this Court as ultimate interpreter of the Constitution."[111] I do not believe that Scalia's statement about "our former constitutional system"[112] is merely hyperbolic. And I believe that Madison would fully concur.

In *Mistretta v. United States* (1989), the Court ratified another of Congress's "complicated and indirect" schemes to aggrandize power to itself. Again, on the face of the matter, Congress seems to be engaged in another act of "self-effacement." In the past, Congress, in delegating power, had to calculate whether the delegation was worth the increase in executive power that the delegation would inevitably entail. However, Congress has now found a way to delegate legislative power without increasing the power of the executive branch; and the Court has ratified this concept as a logical outgrowth of the *Morrison* decision.

In 1984 Congress passed the Sentencing Reform Act, creating a Sentencing Commission to set guidelines for federal crimes. The commission was established as "an independent commission in the judicial branch." The commission has seven voting members, three of whom must be federal judges. They are nominated by the president from a list of six recommendations presented by the Judicial Conference of the United States. The president's nominees must be confirmed by the Senate. Members of the commissions are removable by the president "only for neglect of duty or malfeasance in office or for other good cause shown."

The Court rejected the contention that the Congress had improperly delegated legislative power to a body constituted within the judicial branch. The Court noted that the commission had been given appropriate guidelines for the exercise of their discretion. While noting that the delegation of legislative power always provokes important questions concerning the separation of powers, the Court nevertheless noted that "our jurisprudence has been driven by a practical understanding that in our increasingly complex society, replete with ever changing and more technical problems, Congress simply cannot do its job absent an ability to delegate power under broad general directives."[113] The Court's indulgence is simply dictated by the realities of the modern administrative state. And this indulgence requires a "flexible understanding of the separation of powers."[114]

The Court does concede that "[a]lthough placed by the Act in the Judicial

Branch, it is not a court and does not exercise judicial power." This does not vitiate the scheme, however, since "[o]ur constitutional principles of separated powers are not violated . . . by mere anomaly or innovation."[115] The anomaly, however, was not sufficiently clarified by Justice Blackmun. As Justice Scalia pointed out—again in a lone dissent—what was at stake in this instance was not a delegation with respect to the execution or the adjudication of the law, but law-making power itself. "In the present case," Scalia wrote, "a pure delegation of legislative power is precisely what we have before us. It is irrelevant whether the standards are adequate, because they are not standards related to the executive or judicial powers; they are, plainly and simply, standards for further legislation."[116] If Scalia is right—as I am convinced he is—this would be a clear and unequivocal violation of the separation of powers. As Scalia notes, "[t]he lawmaking function of the Sentencing Commission is completely divorced from any responsibility for execution of the law or adjudication of private rights under the law."[117]

Under the principle of the separation of powers, any delegation of legislative authority must be couched in terms of the application of the law in particular instances, whether in terms of the execution of the law or in adjudication. This was a principle that was well understood in previous years. Chief Justice John Marshall, for example, writing for the majority in *Fletcher v. Peck* (1810) noted that "[i]t is the peculiar province of the legislative power to prescribe general rules for the government of society; the application of those rules to individuals in society would seem to be the duty of other departments."[118] The Sentencing Commission, placed by the act in the judicial branch, performs neither executive not judicial functions, but it does "prescribe general rules for the government of society." Certainly the principle of the separation of powers as understood by Madison and the other leading Founders is violated by the unwarranted admixture of power. It does, however, allow Congress to delegate without increasing the power of the executive branch. But the dynamic of the separation of powers should force Congress to make this calculation—whether to retain legislative power or to increase the provenance of the executive branch by delegating discretion to determine how the laws are to be applied in particular instances. Execution of the law no less than adjudication involves lawmaking. But discretion in terms of the law's application is fundamentally different from the general lawmaking powers that must be lodged exclusively in the legislative branch. And the separation of powers (at least in its principled understanding before *Mistretta*) rightly discouraged Congress from delegating its responsibilities to other branches.

The Court insists that the delegation of power contained in the Sentencing Reform Act is no more an aggrandizement of congressional power than the independent counsel provision of the Ethics in Government Act was. But this represents a fundamental misunderstanding of the principle of the separation of powers on the part of the Court's majority. The separation of powers is a dynamic that pits "ambition against ambition." Any diminution of the president's power is an augmentation of the power of Congress; and any increase of Congress' power is a diminution of executive power. Congressional power, as Madison well knew, can increase subtly and by insinuation. Justice Blackmun, in his opinion for the majority, indicated that arguments contending that the Sentencing Commission violated the fundamental principle of the separation of powers "prove, at least in this case, to be 'more smoke than fire.' " But in legislative-executive relations, it is virtually certain that where there is smoke there is indeed fire.

NOTES

1 *Second Treatise on Government,* in Peter Laslett, ed., *Two Treatises of Government* (New York: New American Library, 1965), par. 143.

2 1 *Annals of Congress* (Gales and Seaton, ed., 1834), p. 604.

3 The debate in 1793 over executive power between Alexander Hamilton, writing as "Pacificus," and James Madison, writing as "Helvedius," remains the quintessential dispute between two Framers of the Constitution who agreed in principle but who differed about the particular application of the principle.

4 James L. Sundquist, quoted in Ann Stuart Anderson, "A 1787 Perspective on Separation of Powers," in Robert A. Goldwin and Art Kaufman, eds., *Separation of Powers—Does It Still Work?* (Washington, DC: American Enterprise Institute, 1986), p. 138. Sundquist's remark was made in response to the Supreme Court's 1983 decision in *I.N.S. v. Chadha,* discussed below. See also Lloyd Cutler, "To Form a Government," in ibid., p. 2: "The separation of powers between the legislative and executive branches, whatever its merits [at the time of the Founding], has become a structure that almost guarantees stalemate today. As we wonder why we are having such a difficult time making decisions we all know must be made and projecting our power and leadership, we should reflect on whether this is one big reason."

5 *Myers v. U.S.,* 272 U.S. 52, 273 (1926) (Brandeis, J., dissenting).

6 *Congressional Government,* in Arthur S. Link, ed., *The Papers of Woodrow Wilson,* 61 vols. to date (Princeton, NJ: Princeton University Press, 1966–   ), 4:172.

7 *Constitutional Government,* in ibid., 18:106.

8 Ibid.

9 *The Federalist,* No. 14, p. 101. See Charles C. Thach, Jr., *The Creation of the Presidency: 1775–1789* (Baltimore: Johns Hopkins University Press, 1923 [reprinted 1969]), p. 171: "The truth is that the Fathers used the theorists as sources from which to draw arguments rather than specific conclusions. The chief problem of distribution of functions and organization of government was to get a sufficiently strong executive."

10 Douglass Adair, "'That Politics May be Reduced to a Science': David Hume, James Madison, and the Tenth Federalist," in Trevor Colbourn, ed., *Fame and the Founding Fathers: Essays by Douglass Adair* (New York: W. W. Norton, 1974), p. 93.

11 See Maynard Smith, "Reason, Passion, and Political Freedom in *The Federalist*," *Journal of Politics,* 22 (August 1960), p. 525, esp. p. 543.

12 Hume, *A Treatise of Human Nature,* L. A. Selby-Bigge, ed. (Oxford: 1888), Bk. II, pt. III, sec. 3, p. 415.

13 *The Federalist,* No. 49, p. 317.

14 See Robert Eden, "Partisanship and the Constitutional Revolution: The Founders' View is Newly Problematic," in Sarah B. Thurow, ed., *Constitutionalism in Perspective: The United States Constitution in Twentieth Century Politics* (Lanham, MD: University Press of America, 1988), p. 59 ff. and particularly the trenchant criticism at p. 52, n. 5.

15 John Marini, "Bureaucracy and Constitutionalism," in ibid., 119. "Woodrow Wilson . . . in his *Essay on Socialism* could find no principled difference between democracy—as understood by the progressives—and socialism."

16 *The Federalist,* No. 70, pp. 424, 423.

17 *Constitutional Government,* in *The Papers of Woodrow Wilson,* 18:71.

18 Richard Hofstadter, *The American Political Tradition* (New York: Vintage, 1948), pp. 16–17.

19 "The Study of Administration," *Political Science Quarterly,* II (June 1887), p. 210; the same point was made by Frank J. Goodnow in his influential *Politics and Administration* published in 1900: "[The] principle of the separation of powers and authorities has proven . . . to be unworkable as a legal principle." Instead of separated powers, the efficient division in "complex" government is between "Politics and Administration. Politics has to do with policies or expressions of the state will. Administration has to do with the execution of these policies." pp. 15, 18.

20 John Marini, "Bureaucracy and Constitutionalism," p. 122.

21 Ibid., p. 118.

22 Ibid., pp. 120 ff.

23 "The Study of Administration," p. 215.

24 Richard Neustadt, *Presidential Power* (New York: John Wiley & Sons, 1962), p. 33 (emphasis original).

25 Louis Fisher, *The Politics of Shared Power,* 2nd ed. (Washington, DC: Congressional Quarterly Press, 1987), p. 1.

26 Ibid., p. 18.

27 *Buckley v. Valeo,* 424 U.S. 1, 121 (1976). The Court here was echoing Justice Robert Jackson's famous statement in *Youngstown Sheet and Tube Co. v. Sawyer,* 343 U.S. 579, 635 (1952): "While the Constitution diffuses power the better to secure liberty, it also contemplates that practice will integrate the dispersed powers into a workable government. It enjoins upon its branches separateness but interdependence, autonomy but reciprocity. Presidential powers are not fixed but fluctuate, depending upon their disjunction or conjunction with those of Congress . . . "

28 *The Federalist,* No. 68, p. 414.

29 Ibid., No. 70, p. 423.

30 Ibid., No. 72, p. 435.

31 Ibid., No. 75, p. 452.

32 Robert G. Dixon, Jr., "Congress, Shared Administration, and Executive Privilege," in Harvey C. Mansfield, *Congress Against the President* (New York: Praeger Publishers, 1975), p. 139.

33 *The Federalist,* No. 48, p. 309.

34 "Congress, Shared Administration . . . ," p. 123.

35 *The Federalist,* No. 66, 401–402.

36 289 U.S. 515, 530 (1933). *See Springer v. Philippine Islands,* 277 U.S. 189, 201–202 (1928) (Sutherland, J.). "The existence in the [Constitution] of occasional provisions expressly giving to one of the departments powers which by their nature otherwise would fall within the general scope of the authority of another department emphasizes, rather than casts doubt upon, the generally inviolate character" of the separation of powers.

37 See, e.g., *U.S. v. Will,* 449 U.S. 200 (1980) and *Northern Pipeline Co. v. Marathon Pipe Line Co.,* 458 U.S. 50 (1982).

38 *Morrison v. Olson,* 108 S.Ct. 2597, 2620 (1988). "Unlike some of our previous cases . . . this case simply does not pose a 'danger of congressional usurpation of Executive Branch functions.'"

39 Morris P. Fiorina, "Congressional Control of the Bureaucracy: A Mismatch of Incentives and Capabilities," in Lawrence Dodd and Bruce Oppenheimer, eds., *Congress Reconsidered,* 2nd ed. (Washington, DC: Congressional Quarterly Press, 1981), pp. 339, 337; see also Margaret N. Davis, "The Congressional Budget Mess," in Gordon S. Jones and John A. Marini, eds., *The Imperial Congress: Crisis in the Separation of Powers* (New York: Pharos Books, 1988), p. 162: "Responsible budgeting calls for Congress to make choices between two competing goals. On one hand, the deficit must be reduced through either spending reductions or increased taxes. On the other hand, serving the constituents and enhancing reelection prospects is made easier by increasing federal spending in the district and lowering taxes. Congress quite naturally has continued to follow policies that enhance incumbency, even at the expense of the national interest."

40 Ibid., p. 343; Senator Robert Packwood once stated the issue in this manner: "We can delegate powers to the President, then sit back and carp or applaud, depending on whether what he does is popular or unpopular." Quoted in Sotirios A. Barber, *The Constitution and the Delegation of Congressional Power* (Chicago: University of Chicago Press, 1976), p. 4.

41 Fisher, pp. 82–83.

42 Fiorina, p. 340.

43 Ibid.

44 Lawrence C. Dodd, "Congress and the Quest for Power," in Lawrence Dodd and Bruce Openheimer, eds., *Congress Reconsidered* (New York: Praeger Publishers, 1977), p. 278.

45 Ibid., p. 271.

46 Mark B. Liedl, "What is Congress Trying to Hide?" *Wall Street Journal,* August 15, 1989, Sec. A, p. 14, c. 3.

47 See, for example, Anne M. Burford, *Are You Tough Enough? An Insider's View of Washington Power Politics* (New York: McGraw-Hill, 1986).

48 *The Federalist,* No. 48, p. 310.

49 Ibid., No. 51, p. 321.

50 Louis Fisher, "Commentaries and Exchanges on the Budget and Program Administration," in L. Gordon Crovitz and Jeremy Rabkin, eds., *The Fettered Presi-*

dency: Legal Constraints on the Executive Branch (Washington, DC: American Enterprise Institute, 1989), p. 186.

51 Louis Fisher, ''Micromanagement by Congress: Reality and Mythology,'' in ibid., pp. 140–141.

52 Barbara H. Craig, *Chadha: The Story of an Epic Constitutional Struggle* (New York: Oxford University Press, 1988), p. 23.

53 *Chadha v. I.N.S.*, 634 F.2d 408, 425 (1980).

54 Id. at 431.

55 Id. at 432.

56 Id.

57 Id. at 433.

58 *I.N.S. v. Chadha*, 462 U.S. 919, 944 (1983).

59 Id. at 952.

60 Assuming *arguendo* that such a private bill would not be a bill of attainder. Chadha's status as a deportable alien was not changed by the Attorney General's suspension of proceedings. Thus a bill deporting Chadha would not have changed his status and therefore could not be viewed as inflicting punishment.

61 *I.N.S. v. Chadha,* at 964–965.

62 Id. at 972.

63 Id. at 984.

64 E. Donald Elliott, ''INS v. Chadha: The Administrative Constitution, the Constitution, and the Legislative Veto,'' 1983 *Supreme Court Review* (1983), p. 176. In his dissent in *Bowshear v. Synar,* 478 U.S. 714, 761–762 (1986), Justice White wrote, in a remark that could have been penned by Woodrow Wilson, that ''with the advent and triumph of the administrative state and the accompanying multiplication of the tasks undertaken by the Federal Government, the Court has been virtually compelled to recognize that Congress may reasonably deem it 'necessary and proper' to vest some among the broad new array of governmental functions in officers who are free from the partisanship that may be expected of agents wholly dependent upon the President.''

65 *I.N.S. v. Chadha,* at 986.

66 *The Federalist,* No. 47, p. 301.

67 478 U.S. 714, 733–734 (1986).

68 Id. at 733.

69 Id. at 726.

70 Id.

71 *The Federalist,* No. 57, p. 353.

72 *In re Sealed Case,* 838 F.2d 476, 527 (1988) (Bader, J., dissenting).

73 Id. at 487 (quoting U.S. Const. Art. II, §3).

74 Id. (quoting *Young v. United States ex rel. Viutton et Fils S.A.,* 107 S.Ct. 2124, 2141 [1987]).

75 Id. at 488.

76 Id. at 489.

77 Id.

78 *Morrison v. Olson,* 108 S.Ct. 2597, 2611 (1988).

79 Id. at 2619.

80 According to the Act (28 U.S.C. §592(g)(1)), "[t]he Committee on the Judiciary of either House of the Congress, or a majority of majority party members or a majority of all nonmajority party members of either such committee, may request in writing that the Attorney General apply for the appointment of an independent counsel."

81 *Morrison,* at 2624.

82 Id. at 2625.

83 Id.

84 Id. 2609.

85 Id. at 2608 (emphasis added).

86 28 U.S.C. §596(a)(1).

87 28 U.S.C. §596(a)(2).

88 28 U.S.C. §596(a)(3).

89 *Morrison,* at 2608.

90 Id.

91 28 U.S.C. §594(a)(6).

92 28 U.S.C. §594(f).

93 See William French Smith, "Independent Counsel Provisions of the Ethics in Government Act," in Crovitz and Rabkin, eds., *The Fettered Presidency,* p. 259.

94 Gordon Crovitz ("The Criminalization of Politics," in Jones and Marini, eds., *The Imperial Congress,* p. 255) chronicles "an incident . . . that is especially illustrative of the abuses these prosecutors, ultimately accountable only to Congress, can perpetrate against their executive branch targets." The statute of limitations for giving false and misleading information to Congress (for which Olson was under investigation by the independent counsel) is five years. This date occurred after the federal court of appeals had declared the independent counsel provisions of the Ethics in Government Act unconstitutional and during the time it was on appeal to the Supreme Court. As Crovitz relates, "Ms. Morrison was worried that her own status would not be resolved until after the Supreme Court ruled, so she set out to intimidate Olson into waiving his right to claim that the statute of limitations had run out." She threatened to seek a "sealed protective indictment" (a device unknown to Justice Department rules) in order to keep the case alive. "By this concept," Crovitz comments, "she presumably meant that she would ask a grand jury to indict Olson despite her having insufficient evidence under the federal guidelines for prosecutors to seek an indictment." This placed Olson in a cruel dilemma. Under the Ethics in Government Act, he could receive reimbursement for his enormous legal expenses only if he was never indicted. Thus, Olson was easily "blackmailed" into waiving his statute of limitations claim in exchange for assurance that the "protective indictment" would be dropped. As Crovitz notes, "[t]his coercion was especially outrageous because the courts have hesitated to uphold such waivers of statute of limitations" (p. 256). The waiver was approved and a short time after the Supreme Court's decision in *Morrison v. Olson,* Morrison announced that no indictments would be forthcoming because there was insufficient evidence against Olson.

95 *Morrison,* at 2609.

96 Id.

97 Id. at 2610.

98 28 U.S.C. §595(a)(c).
99 *Morrison,* at 2618.
100 Id. at 2619.
101 Id.
102 Id. at 2611.
103 Id.
104 Id. at 2626–2627.
105 Id. at 2628.
106 Id. at 2638.
107 *The Federalist,* No. 48, p. 310.
108 Stephen A. Wolf, "In the Pursuit of Power Without Accountability: How the Independent Counsel Statute is Designed and Used to Undermine the Energy and Independence of the Presidency," 35 *South Dakota Law Review* (1990), p. 9.
109 *Morrison,* at 2637.
110 Id. at 2630.
111 *Baker v. Carr,* 369 U.S. 186, 211 (1962).
112 *Morrison,* at 2631.
113 109 S.Ct. 647, 654 (1989).
114 Id. at 659.
115 Id. at 661.
116 Id. at 679.
117 Id.
118 10 U.S. (6 Cranch) 87, 136 (1810).

Chapter Five

Equal Protection and Personal Rights: The Regime of the "Discrete and Insular Minority"

In 1927 Justice Holmes remarked in his infamous opinion in *Buck v. Bell* that the equal protection clause of the Fourteenth Amendment was "the usual last resort of constitutional arguments."[1] This is, of course, certainly no longer the case. After *Brown v. Board of Education* (1954) the equal protection clause almost became the favored constitutional argument of first resort. I doubt if even Holmes would be surprised by this development. For it is merely the direct reflection of society's ever quickening concern for the implementation of equality. As Tocqueville reminded us in his *Democracy in America,* "[w]hen inequality is the general rule in society the greatest inequalities attract no attention; when everything is more or less level, the slightest variation is noticed. Hence the more equal men are, the more insatiable will be their longing for equality."[2]

There is little doubt that equal protection of the laws is intimately connected to constitutional government. All civil liberties, in one form or another, are traceable to this basic constitutional precept. As a constitutional precept, equal protection of the laws derives its dignity from the fact that it is the conventional reflection of the principles that flow directly from natural human equality. Questions of equal protection thus necessarily invite considerations of first principles, or what used to be known as "regime questions"—those fundamental questions that laid bare the principles of the regime and provided, as it were, the occasions for periodic returns to the origins of the regime.

The Supreme Court's most recent interpretations of the Fourteenth Amendment present serious questions that reach to the foundations of the regime. Since the early 1970s the Court has evidenced a view of the equal protection clause that is fundamentally at odds with the moving principle of the American regime. The Court has come perilously close to converting the doctrine of individual rights—a doctrine presupposed by the whole of the American legal and political tradition—into a doctrine of class rights. It has done this through the resurrection of an idea that for all intents and purposes had been stillborn in 1938: the idea of the "discrete and insular" minority. This doctrine was first propounded in the case of *United States v. Carolene Products Co.*,[3] and in light of its subsequent importance[4] it is necessary to cover ground that has already been well covered but perhaps little understood.

As a result of its *volte face* in 1937, the Supreme Court was confronted with the likelihood of more aggressive actions on the part of both state legislatures and the Congress. It thus began tentatively to develop a doctrine that would allow it to insulate what it regarded as fundamental rights from the legislative process. Whereas the Court was willing to forego its staunch defense of the liberty of contract, it was unwilling to leave the field to Congress and the state legislatures uncontested. In *West Coast Hotel Co. v. Parrish* (1937), Chief Justice Hughes wryly noted that "[l]iberty in each of its phases has its history and connotation." The Court now recognized, he continued, that "[t]he Constitution does not speak of freedom of contract . . . [but of] liberty in a social organization which requires the protection of law against the evils which menace the health, safety, morals, and welfare of the people."[5] Whereas liberty of contract was a "negative" liberty that had worked to disallow the interventions of legislatures, "liberty in a social organization" required the intercession of government and contemplated the enlargement of its sphere of activity. Although liberty of contract was no longer a tenable concept, there were still negative liberties implied in the Constitution's specific restrictions upon the exercise of legislative power. These were primarily contained in the Bill of Rights and the Fourteenth Amendment. Here, then, is where the Court would form its skirmish line. And it was precisely in the context of the attempt to articulate the extent of the residue of negative constitutional liberties that the idea of the "discrete and insular" minority developed.

In the *Carolene Products* case, the Court addressed the question of how far it was willing to go in its deference to legislative authority. The case involved a challenge to the power of Congress to regulate the interstate shipment of adulterated milk under the Filled Milk Act of 1923. As George

Braden remarked, Justice Stone, writing for only a plurality of the Court,

> address[ed] himself to a problem arising out of the use of the presumption of constitutionality as a means of forestalling Due Process Clause attacks on economic legislation. His problem was to make the presumption stick in economic cases without being plagued by it in civil liberties and similar cases.[6]

The Court thus had no difficulty upholding the constitutionality of the act in light of Congress's recently expanded powers to regulate economic activity under the aegis of the commerce clause. The Court presupposed, Justice Stone remarked, that

> regulatory legislation affecting ordinary commercial transactions is not to be pronounced unconstitutional unless in the light of the facts made known or generally assumed it is of such a character as to precludes the assumption that it rests upon some rational basis within the knowledge and experience of the legislators.[7]

Appended to this statement is the famous footnote number four in which Justice Stone attempted to suggest some limits to the scope of the Court's deference, an attempt that at least one observer has labeled "typical judicial indirection":[8]

> There may be a narrower scope for operation of the presumption of constitutionality when legislation appears on its face to be within a specific prohibition of the Constitution, such as those of the first ten amendments, which are deemed equally specific when held to be embraced within the Fourteenth. See *Stromberg v. California*, 283 U.S. 359, 369-70; *Lovell v. Griffin*, 303 U.S. 444, 452.
>
> It is unnecessary to consider now whether legislation which restricts those political processes which can ordinarily be expected to bring about repeal of undesirable legislation, is to be subjected to more exacting judicial scrutiny under the general prohibitions of the Fourteenth Amendment than are most other types of legislation. On restrictions upon the right to vote, see *Nixon v. Herndon*, 273 U.S. 536; *Nixon v. Condon*, 286 U.S. 73; on restraints upon the dissemination of information, see *Near v. Minnesota ex rel. Olson*, 283 U.S. 697, 713-714, 718-720, 722; *Grosjean v. American Press Co.*, 297 U.S. 233; *Lovell v. Griffin, supra;* on interferences with political organizations, see *Stromberg v. California, supra*, 369; *Fiske v. Kansas*, 274 U.S. 357, 373-378; *Herndon v. Lowry*, 301 U.S. 242; and see Holmes, J., in *Gitlow v. New York*, 268 U.S. 652, 673; as to prohibition of peaceable assembly, see *De Jonge v. Oregon*, 299 U.S. 353, 365.
>
> Nor need we enquire whether similar considerations enter into the review of statutes directed at particular religious, *Pierce v. Society of Sisters*, 268 U.S. 510, or national, *Meyer v. Nebraska*, 262 U.S. 390; *Bartels v. Iowa*, 262 U.S. 404; *Farrington v. Tokushige*, 273 U.S. 484, or racial minorities, *Nixon v. Herndon, supra; Nixon v. Condon, supra;* whether prejudice against discrete and insular minorities may be a special condition, which tends seriously to curtail the operation of those political processes ordinarily to be relied upon to protect minorities, and which may call for a correspondingly more searching judicial inquiry. Compare

McCulloch v. Maryland, 4 Wheat. 316, 428; *South Carolina v. Barnwell Bros.,* 303 U.S. 177, 184 n. 2, and cases cited.[9]

In these three terse and enigmatic paragraphs Justice Stone indicated the three general areas that would mark the limit of the Court's willingness to defer to legislative judgment, or at least provide a "narrower scope for . . . the presumption of constitutionality." The meaning of the first paragraph is clear enough in terms of constitutional construction: any legislation that impinges upon specific constitutional prohibitions, particularly those contained in the Bill of Rights, and by extension the Fourteenth Amendment would not be viewed as presumptively valid. Since these rights are specifically insulated from legislative encroachments, it is the special province of the Supreme Court to apply a narrower scope of presumptive constitutionality in cases where legislation touches upon those rights, regardless of the representative character of the legislation or the class status of those whose rights might be affected. It is the character of the rights, not the character of the representation, that determines the application of the "narrower scope." The two cases cited as authority— *Stromberg* and *Lovell*—were cases in which Chief Justice Hughes had written majority opinions striking down state laws that encroached upon First Amendment freedoms, which were described as "fundamental." These rights, Justice Jackson later noted in his majority opinion in *West Virginia State Board of Education v. Barnette,* "may not be submitted to vote; they depend on the outcome of no elections."[10]

It has been noted that whereas the first paragraph deals with fundamental rights "within the scope of specific constitutional prohibitions," the second two paragraphs "refer to political processes."[11] The second paragraph addresses itself to the integrity of the majoritarian political process and the third to the protection of minorities—the twin problems of democratic government treated so assiduously by *The Federalist.* Legislation that invades the democratic process, Stone intimates, would be viewed as presumptively invalid since such invasions would debase the idea of democratic government itself.

Many commentators have argued that there is a lack of consistency between the first two paragraphs, the first paragraph indicating that certain rights are to be protected because they are specifically insulated from the political process, and the second paragraph noting that these *same* rights are to be protected because they are an indispensable part of the democratic process.[12] In fact, the overlapping references in all three paragraphs might, at first glance, seem inapposite. Almost all of the cases cited in the second paragraph were cited either in the first paragraph or in the cases cited therein. The only major additions are the *Herndon* and *Condon* cases cited as authority for the protection of voting rights under the "general prohibitions of the Fourteenth Amendment." These cases invalidated state primary laws excluding blacks, and both fall within the scope of the rights covered in the first paragraph.

These overlapping references indicate that the second two paragraphs of the note were intended to be read as glosses on the first paragraph. Any legislation impinging upon the democratic process is subject to "more exacting judicial scrutiny" because the democratic process is the vehicle or means for securing "fundamental rights." Similarly, as seen in the later discussion of paragraph three, legislation directed specifically at religious or racial minorities is *a priori* a "special condition" that triggers solicitude for those rights that are insulated from the majoritarian political process. Part of the confusion stems from the fact that the rights guaranteed by the Fourteenth Amendment have a twofold character. They are both ends in themselves and instrumental to the maintenance of democratic government. Thus we have the seeming dilemma that those rights guaranteeing participation in the democratic process cannot be infringed by the democratic process itself. And it is this twofold aspect of the rights in question that accounts for the overlapping references. Religious freedom, for example, would be less an instrumental right than voting. Religious freedom *is* instrumental to democratic government but not in the same sense as voting, which seems almost to be exclusively procedural or instrumental. Yet voting *is* "a fundamental political right, because [it is] preservative of all rights."[13]

In the crucial third paragraph Justice Stone implies that "exacting judicial scrutiny" might be called for in "the review of statutes directed at particular religious . . . or national . . . or racial minorities." Once again, Stone cites *Herndon* and *Condon*. The primary laws invalidated in these cases not only interfered with political rights intimately connected to the democratic process, but were directed exclusively at a racial minority. Their citation in paragraph two indicates that the statutes would have been invalidated even if there had been no racial classification involved. The fact that both cases were disposed of under the Fourteenth Amendment, rather than the Fifteenth, also suggests this clearly enough. Still, legislation directed at racial minorities in the manner of these primary laws will be viewed as presumptively invalid because any classification based on race creates a "special condition" that calls forth solicitude for fundamental Fourteenth Amendment rights.

Everything to this point seems to partake of some semblance of order. The final citations, illustrating "prejudice against discrete and insular minorities . . . which tends seriously to curtail the operation of those political processes ordinarily to be relied upon to protect minorities," seem, however, to be rather curious. *McCulloch v. Maryland,* the first case cited, is, of course, Chief Justice Marshall's great defense of national sovereignty. The particular reference made by Justice Stone is to that part of Marshall's opinion delineating the superiority of national majorities to local state majorities. The power to tax, Marshall argued, is a sovereign prerogative of government and the only security against its abuse is "the structure of the government itself. In imposing a tax the legislature acts upon its constituents. This is in general a sufficient security against erroneous and oppressive taxation."[14] But in the case of a state legislature taxing an instrumentality of the federal government, the security that proceeds from "the structure of government" is unavailable since the nation as a whole is not represented in the state legislature. Marshall concluded that since state legislatures are not representative of the whole, they therefore cannot legislate for the whole.

South Carolina State Highway Department v. Barnwell Brothers, the second case cited, was decided the same term as *Carolene Products,* with Justice Stone also writing the majority opinion. In *Barnwell,* a South Carolina law that limited the size and weight of trucks traveling within the state was challenged as imposing "an unconstitutional burden upon interstate commerce."[15] Justice Stone remarked that the lower court had "proceeded upon the assumption that the commerce clause imposes upon state regulations to secure the safe and economical use of highways a standard of reasonableness which is more exacting when applied to the interstate traffic than that required by the Fourteenth Amendment as to all traffic."[16] And, appropriately enough, tucked away in a footnote is an explanation of the independent force of the commerce clause "to curtail state power in some measure" in the absence of congressional action."

> State regulations affecting interstate commerce, whose purpose or effect is to gain for those within the state an advantage at the expense of those without, or to burden those out of the state without any corresponding advantage to those within, have been thought to impinge upon the constitutional prohibition even though Congress has not acted.[17]

Continuing the footnote, Justice Stone used language similar to that which appeared later in the term in the *Carolene Products* footnote:

> Underlying the stated rule has been the thought, often expressed in judicial opinion, that when the regulation is of such a character that its burden falls principally upon those without the state, legislative action is not likely to be subjected to *those political restraints which are normally exerted on legislation where it affects adversely some interests within the state.*[18]

Thus if the burden of state regulation falls principally on those not represented by the state legislature that imposes the burden, this "impinge[s] upon the constitutional prohibition even though Congress has not acted."[19]

From the two citations—*McCulloch* and *Barnwell*—it is clear that Justice Stone meant to include in "discrete and insular minorities" those who are unreasonably disadvantaged by laws passed by legislatures that do not represent them. The "discreteness" and "insularity" proceed precisely from this lack of representation. The question here is whether Stone meant to suggest that religious and racial minorities were "discrete and insular minorities" in the sense of *McCulloch* and *Barnwell.* Racial and religious groups, of course, are not alienated from the political process in the same way, and although their minority status might always preclude them from dominating *as a minority,* this certainly does not imply that their interests are not represented in the democratic process or that they are not a part of that process.

The only other time Justice Stone used the phrase "discrete and insular minorities" was in his dissent in *Minersville School District v. Gobitis* (1940). After quoting the *Carolene Products* injunction that "prejudice against discrete and insular minorities may tend to curtail the operation of those political processes ordinarily to be relied onto protect minorities," he remarked that "*until now* we have not hesitated similarly to scrutinize legislation restricting the civil liberty of racial and religious minorities *although no political process was affected.*"[20] The Constitution, in Stone's view, was offended because the state legislature had violated "specific constitutional restrictions"[21] contained within the Fourteenth Amendment.

Religious and racial minorities are obviously not alienated from the political process in the same way as the unrepresented groups described in *McCulloch* and *Barnwell*. Not being able to dominate the representative process in terms of religious or racial interests is not the same or the equivalent, as many would argue, of not being represented at all. Religious and racial groups that find themselves in a situation roughly analogous to the groups described in *McCulloch* and *Barnwell* with respect to specific First or Fourteenth Amendment rights do, however, exhibit a "special condition . . . which may call for . . . more searching judicial inquiry." Here the more exacting scrutiny will be in the service of constitutional rights that are independent of the representative process. From this point of view, Stone's note in *Carolene Products* must properly be viewed as a tentative statement of what later came to be known as the "strict scrutiny" test. There is no evidence that he had any intention of giving procedural rights an independent constitutional status, as some would argue.[22]

As we will see, today's reliance on *Carolene Products'* footnote four has gone far beyond the cautious and enigmatic pronouncements made by Justice Stone, who seems not to have worked out any consistent theory of representation but to have made only some tentative suggestions regarding the level of judicial scrutiny that would apply in "special conditions." Justice Frankfurter complained in 1949 in *Kovacs v. Cooper* that a "footnote hardly seems to be an appropriate way of announcing a new constitutional doctrine, and the *Carolene* footnote did not purport to announce any new doctrine; incidentally, it did not have the concurrence of a majority of the Court."[23] My own extended treatment of an "otherwise obscure case"[24] would not be warranted except for the great importance which has been attached to it in recent years.[25]

Although the *Carolene Products* footnote was used several times in the 1940s as authority for the Court's efforts to establish First Amendment freedoms as "preferred freedoms,"[26] nothing more was heard about "discrete and insular minorities" as a "special condition" calling for "more searching judicial inquiry" until 1970, when it was fittingly referred to in a footnote in the case of *Oregon v. Mitchell.* This case involved a 1970 federal voting rights statute that lowered the minimum voting age for both state and federal elections from twenty-one to eighteen. Justice Stewart noted in passing:

> [i]t is inconceivable . . . that this Court would ever hold that the denial of the vote to those between the ages of 18 and 21 constitutes such an invidious discrimination as to be a denial of the equal protection of the laws. The establishment of an age qualification is not state action aimed at any discrete and insular minority.[27]

Thus the "modern" career of the "discrete and insular" minority began. Here was a group that was certainly alienated from the majoritarian political process, but as Stewart seems to indicate, the alienation did not amount to an invidious discrimination under the equal protection clause.

The next year, Chief Justice Burger, writing for the majority in *Gordon v. Lance,* upheld provisions of the West Virginia Constitution that required a sixty percent majority in referendum elections to approve bonded indebtedness and tax increases. "[T]he West Virginia Constitution," Burger stated, "singles out no 'discrete and insular minority' for special treatment. The three-fifths requirement applies equally to all bond issues for any purpose, whether for schools, sewers, or highways."[28]

Both of these cases presented claims involving the quality of representation in the democratic political process and, as such, applied the phrase "discrete and insular minority" in a manner consistent with Justice Stone's use of *McCulloch* and *Barnwell* in the *Carolene Products* footnote.

The Court, however, was not slow in seeing other possibilities suggested by *Mitchell* and *Gordon.* In the 1971 case of *Graham v. Richardson,* the Court for the first time identified a "discrete and insular" minority and used the concept to invalidate legislation under the equal protection clause. *Graham* struck down state welfare laws that conditioned eligibility for state welfare benefits on citizenship or residency for a specified number of years. Justice Blackmun, writing for a unanimous court, noted a line of cases establishing "that classifications based on alienage, like those based on nationality or race, are inherently suspect and subject to close judicial scrutiny. Aliens as a class are a prime example of a 'discrete and insular' minority for whom such heightened judicial solicitude is appropriate."[29] Aliens, although receiving the protection of the Fourteenth Amendment, are not, unlike racial and nationality groups, part of the majoritarian political process. As such, aliens, it might be argued, would fit Justice Stone's original definition of the "discrete and insular" minority, and any laws classifying on the basis of alienage should thus be subject to "more searching judicial inquiry."

After *Graham* the Court was inundated by a veritable flood of claims for "discrete and insular" minority status. The bulk of the cases involved claims that succeeded in overturning a variety of laws classifying on the basis of alienage.[30] The Court refused, however, to extend such class status to illegitimates,[31] the poor,[32] and conscientious objectors.[33] Oddly enough, it was not until fairly recently that race has been explicitly denominated by a majority of the Court as a class characteristic supporting "discrete and insular" minority status.

Justice Marshall was thus exaggerating when he wrote in his dissent in *San Antonio Independent School District v. Rodriguez* (1973) that:

> The highly suspect character of classifications based on race, nationality, or alienage is well established. The reasons why such classifications call for close judicial scrutiny are manifold. Certain racial and ethnic groups have frequently been recognized as "discrete and insular minorities" who are relatively powerless to protect their interests in the political process.[34]

Justice Marshall here speaks of racial and ethnic groups that are "relatively powerless" to protect their interests. These are not groups who are disenfranchised—such as aliens—but groups that participate in, but do not control, the majoritarian political process. It is not political powerlessness as such, according to Marshall, but relative disadvantage resulting from "historic experiences with oppression . . . and discrimination" that identify the "discrete and insular" minority.[35] Although Justice Powell, writing for the majority, disagreed with Marshall respecting the particular claim at issue, he did agree with him about the identity of the "discrete and insular" minority.

> The system of alleged discrimination and the class it defines have none of the traditional indicia of suspectness: the class is not saddled with such disabilities, or subjected to such a history of purposeful unequal treatment, or relegated to such a position of political powerlessness as to command extraordinary protection from the majoritarian political process.[36]

Thus "political powerlessness" is not necessarily the defining characteristic of the "discrete and insular" minority. It also includes "historic" discrimination. This added dimension of "historic" discrimination or "traditional indicia" puts the concept of the "discrete and insular" minority on considerably vaguer grounds. As Justice Rehnquist noted:

> Our society, consisting of over 200 million individuals of multitudinous origins, customs, tongues, beliefs, and cultures is, to say the least, diverse. It would hardly take extraordinary ingenuity for a lawyer to find "discrete and insular" minorities at every turn in the road. Yet, unless the Court can precisely define and constitutionally justify both the terms and analysis it uses . . . the Court can choose [any] "minority" it "feels" deserves "solicitude." . . . [37]

We might add that, under the conditions described by Justice Rehnquist, it is almost impossible to determine whether a group is a "discrete and insular" minority or whether it is merely one that has lost in the political process.[38]

Regents of the University of California v. Bakke (1978) presented the question of the "discrete and insular" minority in a new light. Since 1971 the Court had used the idea to trigger "heightened judicial solicitude" whenever a law impinged upon the equal protection rights of such groups. The question now, however, was whether the same "solicitude" should be applied to test a governmental action designed to benefit rather than injure a "discrete and insular" minority. The university had failed to persuade the California Supreme Court that the racial classification in its special admissions program served a compelling state interest under traditional strict scrutiny analysis. The strategy then became to induce the Supreme Court to apply a less exacting test in light of the "benign" purpose of the classification and in light of the fact that the injury induced by the classification was not an injury to a member of a "discrete and insular" minority. The university used *Carolene Products* as its authority for arguing that the "strict scrutiny" test was reserved exclusively for "discrete and insular minorities." Four members of the Court (Brennan, White, Marshall, and Blackmun in their "joint separate opinion") agreed with the university, arguing that members of the majority needed no protection from the majoritarian political process that authorized the actions of the university.

Justice Powell, however, rejected this ploy, remarking that:

> The guarantees of the Fourteenth Amendment extend to all persons. . . . It is settled beyond question that the "rights created by the . . . Fourteenth Amendment are, by its terms, guaranteed to the individual. The rights established are personal rights. . . ." The guarantee of equal protection cannot mean one thing when applied to one individual and something else when applied to a person of another color. . . .
>
>   . . . Nor has this Court held that discreteness and insularity constitute necessary preconditions to a holding that a particular classification is invidious.[39]

Powell further stated that "discreteness" and "insularity" might be "characteristics" relevant to a consideration of whether or not to add new classes to "the list of 'suspect' categories or whether a particular classification survives close examination," but neither has ever been held to be the exclusive precondition for close scrutiny. Race, in contrast, is a classification that automatically triggers "strict scrutiny," and no action based on a racial classification has survived "strict scrutiny" since *Korematsu v. United States,* the Japanese exclusion case decided in 1944. As Powell rightly noted, the language of "suspect classifications" was first used in *Korematsu,* where Justice Black, writing for the majority, remarked:

> It should be noted, to begin with, that all legal restrictions which curtail the civil rights of a single racial group are immediately suspect. This is not to say that all such restrictions are unconstitutional. It is to say that courts must subject them to the most rigid scrutiny. Pressing public necessity may sometimes justify the existence of such restrictions; racial antagonism never can.[40]

As is well known, *Korematsu* upheld the constitutionality of the racial classification as "a pressing public necessity" dictated by the "conditions of modern warfare."[41] And, by all accounts, it was a decision the Court regretted until it has now come to be used as an *authority* for the proposition that the court has never—and is not required to—interpret the Constitution in a "colorblind" manner!

The development of strict scrutiny analysis was an attempt by the Court to refine the "reasonableness" test that had traditionally served as the standard for legislative classifications. The necessity of classification in legislation is evident. Every law treats different classes of people differently. Quite clearly, equal protection of the laws does not demand that everyone be treated equally but only those who are similarly situated, i.e., in the same class. The test is whether the classification created by the law is a reasonable one in light of some constitutional purpose. And, as has often been noted, the "reasonableness" test has given wide discretion to legislatures, as is no doubt appropriate for a democratic regime.[42]

The "strict scrutiny" test, in contrast, presumes that classifications based on race or religion or those that impinge upon fundamental rights are *ipso facto* unreasonable and therefore arbitrary. It is an *a priori* assumption that neither race nor religion can be the basis for legitimate classifications in a liberal regime, a regime that has as its sole legitimating purpose the protection of individual rights. Professor Gunther attempted to show the inefficacy of this two-tiered test of legislative classification when he wrote, in a much quoted passage, that "strict scrutiny" was "'strict' in theory and fatal in fact,'" whereas the "reasonableness' test provided "minimum scrutiny in theory and virtually none in fact."[43] But "reasonableness' and "strict scrutiny" are really two aspects of the same test. "Strict scrutiny" merely presumes that some classifications—particularly those based on race or religion—are unreasonable. This "two-tiered test" is simply the recognition that in liberal societies reason must replace will as the foundation of the laws, and that declarations as to what is reasonable are generally the province of legislatures. That "strict scrutiny" is nearly always fatal in fact is, I believe, an irrefragable expression of the kind of liberalism that the Court now seems so eager to abandon—and does abandon in *Metro Broadcasting v. FCC* (1990).

In rejecting the university's claim in *Bakke* that the equal protection clause should not be invoked to protect the rights of a member of the white majority, Justice Powell, paraphrasing *Brown v. Board of Education,* laconically noted: "The clock of our liberties . . . cannot be turned back to 1868. . . . It is far too late to argue that the guarantee of equal protection to *all* persons permits the recognition of special wards entitled to a degree of protection greater than that accorded to others."[44] Such a dilution of the strict dictates of equal protection, Powell argued, would make "constitutional principles" depend on "transitory considerations," creating a situation where "judicial scrutiny of classifications touching on racial and ethnic background may vary with the ebb and flow of political forces.''[45] Such an interpretation as the university urged upon the Court—and the one accepted by Brennan et al.—would convert the Fourteenth Amendment's equal protection clause into one protecting classes exclusively and not, as Powell correctly believed its framers intended, one designed to minimize the role of classes by emphasizing the protection of individuals.

Indeed the university and the four dissenters in their joint separate opinion would have reinterpreted the equal protection clause so as to convert it into an instrument of class remedies for what are deemed to be essentially class injuries. As Justice Marshall remarked in his separate opinion, '[i]t is unnecessary in 20th-century America to have individual Negroes demonstrate that they have been victims of racial discrimination; the racism of our society has been so pervasive that none, regardless of wealth or position, has managed to escape its impact.''[46] But this class analysis, as Powell points out, necessarily ignores individuals and the rights that adhere to individuals, rather than classes. Class analysis paints with a broad brush that necessarily abstracts from the differing situations of the individuals who make up the class. In a case handed down just two months before the *Bakke* decision, the Court remarked that "[e]ven a true generalization about the class is an insufficient reason for disqualifying an individual to whom the generalization does not apply." Although the Court here was concerned with the Civil Rights Act of 1964, its analysis of the role of class in liberal jurisprudence was correct: liberalism "precludes treatment of individuals as simply components of a racial, religious, sexual or national class."[47]

The intrusion of class brings into question the very idea of liberal jurisprudence. Such jurisprudence finds its basis in the moral obligations of individual human beings. As Professor Arkes has noted, the attribute of individual moral responsibility is the distinct mark of human nature and the premise of law itself. For without the assumption of some essential moral responsibility on the part of individuals, there could be no place for the concepts of jurisprudence and citizenship. Jurisprudence must assume that individuals can be held responsible for their own acts, and this assumption would hardly be warranted if human beings did not have sufficient freedom to form their own acts and reach judgments over matters of right and wrong.[48]

Indeed, a great principle of liberal jurisprudence holds that whenever the law has created an injury, the law must afford a remedy. The accepted formula is that "the one whose primary right has been violated immediately acquires a secondary right to obtain an appropriate remedy from the wrongdoer, while the wrongdoer himself becomes subjected to the secondary duty of giving or suffering such remedy."[49] But a necessary concomitant of this principle is that no one can be made a part of the remedy who has not been a part of the injury. Both of these precepts derive from the presumption that the individual is the recipient of the rights in question. Class remedies, however, give remedies to individuals whose rights have not necessarily been violated and injure those who are innocent of having perpetrated any injury by making them part of the remedy. Thus the correspondence between injury and remedy, which is at the heart of liberal jurisprudence, becomes totally arbitrary. As Justice Powell explained: "[T]here is a measure of inequity in forcing innocent persons in respondent's position to bear the burdens of redressing grievances not of their making."[50] Using class considerations as a means of fashioning equitable remedies for such injuries as "historic" discrimination or "the present effects of past discrimination" will inevitably destroy the possibility of a jurisprudence based on constitutional principles. It is only by viewing the equal protection clause as the guarantor of individual rights, Powell argued, that the Constitution can ultimately be applied in a nonarbitrary manner.

> If it is the individual who is entitled to judicial protection against classifications based upon his racial or ethnic background because such distinctions impinge upon personal rights, rather than the individual only because of his membership in a particular group, then constitutional standards may be applied consistently. Political judgments regarding the necessity for the particular classifications may be weighted in the constitutional balance . . . but the standard of justification will remain constant. This is as it should be, since those political judgments are the product of rough compromise struck by contending groups within the democratic process. When they touch upon an individual's race or ethnic background, he is entitled to a judicial determination that the burden he is asked to bear on that basis is precisely tailored to serve a compelling governmental interest. The Constitution guarantees that right to every person regardless of his background.[51]

As Powell pointed out, an adherence to a conception of equal protection that disallows class considerations is the only one possible that is consistent with the dictates of principled constitutional government. Anything else simply makes protection of constitutional rights "vary with the ebb and flow of political forces."[52]

If, for example, the Court were forced to choose between the claims of competing classes, what standards would it use to adjudicate the competing claims? Would it rely on the relative degree of "historic" discrimination? Or say that some "traditional indicia" are more significant that others? Or what? As Powell pointed out, more than likely the claims would be resolved by the prevailing political forces and not by any constitutional principles.

The Court was confronted with the issue of competing claims in 1977 in *United Jewish Organizations v. Carey*. Acting under section five of the Voting Rights Act of 1965, the Justice Department found that New York had failed to demonstrate with respect to one county that its proposed redistricting plan was nondiscriminatory. The state responded to the objections by submitting a revised plan that created "more 'substantial nonwhite majorities'" in four of the county's districts.[53] In order to accomplish this, New York had found it necessary to divide an Hasidic Jewish community previously contained in a single district. The Hasidim complained that reapportionment that proceeded from explicitly racial considerations violated the equal protection clause and the Fifteenth Amendment. The Court, however, disallowed the claim that reapportionment within the remedial scope of section five had to be racially neutral. Justice White announced the judgment of the Court and, in a part of his opinion joined by Justice Stevens and Justice Rehnquist, argued that the use of race here was not objectionable because it "represented no racial slur or stigma with respect to whites or any other race. . . . [T]here was no fencing out of the white population from participation in the political process of the county, and the plan did not minimize or unfairly cancel out white voting strength."[54] Although the United Jewish Organizations did not press a claim based on their class status, Justice Brennan indicated how the Court would have decided in that instance:

> [W]hen interpreting the broad principles embraced by the Equal Protection Clause, we cannot well ignore the social reality that even a benign policy of assignment by race is viewed as unjust by many in our society, especially by those individuals who are adversely affected by a given classification. This impression of injustice may be heightened by the natural consequence of our governing processes that the most "discrete and insular" of whites often will be called upon to bear the immediate, direct costs of benign discrimination.[55]

How one decides which "discrete and insular" minority is to bear the burden admits, of course, of no constitutional standards. What seems sufficient here is that the Hasidim could be subsumed within the class "whites" and that no "stigma" could be attached to them as members of that class.

> [T]he obvious remedial nature of the Act and its enactment by an elected Congress that hardly can be viewed as dominated by nonwhite representatives belie the possibility that the decisionmaker intended a racial insult or injury to those whites who are adversely affected by the operation of the Act's provisions.[56]

This last quotation with its suggestion that the majority cannot injure or "stigmatize" itself as class has become an important concept in recent cases, particularly *Weber* and *Fullilove*. If it can be determined that legislative intent was remedial in a racial context, then individual members of the majority cannot claim injury because it is a kind of self-imposed injury, or at least not an injury suffered at the hands of others. What, we wonder, would the Court decide in the situation where a group exhibiting all "the traditional indicia of suspectness" actually constituted a majority in a certain political context and discriminated against itself through the majoritarian political process? Impossible? Not at all. In 1977, the same year as the *United Jewish Organizations* case, the Court decided the case of *Castaneda v. Partida*.

Although *Castaneda* has been little noticed, it is nevertheless quite revealing. The case arose in Hildago County, Texas, a county whose population was 79.1 percent Mexican-American according to the 1970 census. Rodrigo Partida was convicted of burglary with intent to rape, and he appealed, alleging a violation of equal protection because in the eleven-year period preceding his indictment and conviction, only 39 percent of those summoned for grand jury service were Mexican-American, and only 50 percent impaneled at the time of his indictment were Mexican-American. Three of the five grand jury commissioners who selected prospective grand jurors, as well as the trial judge and the Federal District Court judge who heard the first federal challenge, were Mexican-American.

It is a rule of long standing that any purposeful racial discrimination in the selection of jurors is a violation of the Fourteenth Amendment, and the court has even allowed challenges to the purposeful exclusion of races other than the one of the person on trial.[57] But it is also the rule that, absent purposeful racial exclusion, a defendant is not guaranteed proportional racial representation—or even any racial representation—in the juries actually impaneled. Significant disproportionality, of course, places the burden of proof of nondiscrimination on the state. The state in the *Castaneda* case did not bear the burden of proof because it did not believe, given the fact that the "ruling majority" in the county was Mexican-American, that there was anything to prove. Here, the Court was faced with a question that was bound to arise once it began to speak in terms of "discrete and insular" minorities: what happens in a case where the group having all the "traditional indicia of suspectness" *dominates* the majoritarian political process? If it treated this majority the same way it treated the "dominant white majority," the Court would merely say that such discrimination against the majority by the majority presented no Fourteenth Amendment claims because, evidently, the discrimination did not eventuate from the powerlessness of the group experiencing the discrimination nor was it suffered at the hands of "others." Whatever individual or isolated injuries might have occurred—as in the case of Rodrigo Partida—would have to be viewed as unobjectionable because they did not result from discrimination by a majority of another race and therefore did not involve racial "stigma."

The Court, however, did not follow this line of argument but, instead, adopted one that, although almost unparalleled for its ingenuousness, was calculated to save the concept of the "discrete and insular" minority. A "discrete and insular" minority—one, that is, with the "traditional indicia"—did not lose its "discreteness" and "insularity," the Court argued, by becoming a "governing majority." Justice Blackmun, writing for the majority, skirted the issue nicely:

The relevance of a governing majority of elected officials to the grand jury selection process is questionable. The fact that certain elected officials are Mexican-American demonstrates nothing about the motivations and methods of the grand jury commissioners who select persons for grand jury lists. . . . [T]hree of the five jury commissioners in respondent's case were Mexican-American. Knowing only this, we would be forced to rely on the reasoning that we have rejected—that human beings would not discriminate against their own kind—in order to find that the presumption of purposeful discrimination was rebutted.[58]

But this is precisely the reasoning that was relied upon in *United Jewish Organizations* and, for all intents and purposes, the cases in which the Court ascribes "benign" racial purposes to congressional enactments.

Justice Marshall, in his concurring opinion, was not quite so circumspect as he engaged in a dialectical exchange with Justice Powell, who dissented. Powell had remarked that:

> In these circumstances, where Mexican-Americans control both the selection of jurors and the political process, rational inferences from the most basic facts in a democratic society render improbable respondent's claim of an intent to discriminate against him and other Mexican-Americans. As [Federal District Court] Judge Garza observed: "If people in charge can choose whom they want, it is unlikely they will discriminate against themselves."[59]

Marshall, however, did not find Powell's "assumptions about human nature" consistent with current "social science theory and research."

> Social scientists agree that members of minority groups frequently respond to discrimination and prejudice by attempting to disassociate themselves from the group, even to the point of adopting the majority's negative attitudes towards the minority. Such behavior occurs with particular frequency among members of minority groups who have achieved some measure of economic or political success and thereby have gained some acceptability among the dominant group.[60]

Thus Marshall—and this is also implicit in Blackmun's rejection of the "governing majority" theory—maintains that "discreteness" and "insularity" are the permanent conditions of those groups with the "traditional indicia of suspectness." Those minorities who do become majorities simply become indistinguishable parts of the "monolithic" white majority. Thus power, no matter who exercises it, will express the ideology of the white majority and, it seems, will always be directed against "discrete and insular" minorities.

It should be clear from this analysis of *United Jewish Organizations* and *Castaneda* that Powell's argument in *Bakke* is correct. The intrusion of class into equal protection analysis makes any principled application of the Fourteenth Amendment impossible. Equal protection can be the foundation of a genuinely thoroughgoing liberal jurisprudence only if it applies to individuals. As I think the framers of both the Fourteenth Amendment and the Constitution certainly knew, class politics is not compatible with constitutional government. Powell persuasively argued in *Bakke* that the Court had never approved a remedy based on race absent "clearly determined constitutional violations" and a clear demonstration of individual injury. This had been true of both desegregation and employment discrimination cases, where the "[r]acial classifications thus were designed as remedies for the vindication of constitutional entitlement."[61] Brennan et al. argued—an argument that the majority opinion in later cases, most notably *Weber,* and *Fullilove*—not for the vindication of discernable constitutional rights, but of unspecified past discriminations of which Bakke admittedly was not a part. The only way Bakke could be said to have been a part of these unspecified injuries that resulted in racial disproportion in California's medical schools is if all members of Bakke's racial class are deemed to be guilty of all past discrimination and the present effects of past discrimination regardless of their individual actions. Absent such reasoning, it is impossible to argue that Bakke had not been injured by the actions of the university.[62]

Brennan et al., however, preferred not to speak of injury but of "stigma." Stigma has emerged as the new standard of the new equal protection. As the joint separate opinion in *Bakke* noted, drawing on the passage from Professor Gunther quoted earlier, "our review under the Fourteenth Amendment should be strict—not 'strict in theory and fatal in fact,' *because it is stigma that causes fatality*—but strict and searching nonetheless."[63] Although individuals such as Bakke are "injured" by racial classifications, the injuries are not the kind that "stigmatize" because, as the joint separate opinion maintains in language that has been steadily making its way to majority status since 1973, "whites as a class have [none] of the 'traditional indicia of suspectness: the class is not saddled with such disabilities, or subjected to such a history of purposeful unequal treatment, or relegated to such a position of political powerlessness as to command extraordinary protection from the majoritarian political process.'"[64] Although Bakke may have been injured in other ways by the racial classifications, he was not branded as a member of an "inferior" race. And it is only the latter that is rendered suspect by the Fourteenth Amendment, the joint opinion argued, if the classification has an otherwise "benign" racial purpose.

The language of "stigma," of course, stems directly from *Brown v. Board of Education* (1954). *Brown* is widely celebrated as the case that finally overruled the "separate but equal" doctrine of *Plessy v. Ferguson* (1896). But one of the most curious aspects of the *Brown* decision is that it does not once refer to Justice Harlan's celebrated dissent in *Plessy.* Harlan's ringing phrases had served for more than fifty years as the focal point of the kind of activist liberalism that the Warren Court would eventually come to epitomize:

> Our Constitution is color-blind, and neither knows nor tolerates classes among citizens. In respect of civil rights, all citizens are equal before the law. The humblest is the peer of the most powerful. The law regards man as man, and takes no account of his surroundings or of his color when his civil rights as guaranteed by the supreme law of the land are involved. It is, therefore, to be regretted that this high tribunal, the final expositor of the fundamental law of the land, has reached the conclusion that it is competent for a State to regulate the enjoyment by citizens of their civil rights solely upon the basis of race.[65]

Instead of merely remarking that the state classification based on race could serve no "compelling state interest" and was for that reason unconstitutional, Chief Justice Warren undertook to prove why racial classifications were suspect and therefore presumed arbitrary from the point of view of the Constitution. But the ground he chose for this proof is startling; it is not that of Harlan's dissent, but the wholly subjective one of the *Plessy* majority:

> To separate [school children] solely because of their race generates a feeling of inferiority as to their status in the community that may affect their hearts and minds in a way unlikely to be undone . . . Whatever may have been the extent of psychological knowledge at the time of *Plessy v. Ferguson,* this finding is amply supported by modern authority. Any language in *Plessy v. Ferguson* contrary to this finding is rejected.[66]

Justice Brown, writing for the majority in *Plessy* in 1896, had stated:

> We consider the underlying fallacy of the plaintiff's argument to consist in the assumption that the enforced separation of the two races stamps the colored race with a badge of inferiority. If this be so, it is not by reason of anything found in the act, but solely because the colored race chooses to put that construction upon it.[67]

Thus it is clear that *Brown* rests upon the same ground of interpretation as *Plessy.* The real defect of *Plessy,* Warren implied, was inadequate knowledge of psychology, not the application of defective principles of constitutional construction. Is there a stigma implied in the separation of the races? Absent any such stigma, even on the basis of *Brown,* the Constitution is not offended. As Warren noted, "*in the field of public education* the doctrine of 'separate but equal' has no place."[68] Other cases—*Brown's* progeny—have extended this holding to other areas, but always, it seems clear, upholding the principle of *Plessy.* Contrary to common opinion, *Brown* did not overrule the *Plessy* decision *tout court;* separate but equal, as recent cases upholding race-conscious classifications demonstrate, is still good constitutional law.

This conclusion is amply supported by the joint separate opinion in *Bakke:* "no decision of this Court has ever adopted the proposition that the Constitution must be colorblind."[69] Indeed, the opinion continues,

> [t]he assertion of human equality is closely associated with the proposition that differences in color or creed, birth or status, are nether significant nor relevant to the way in which persons should be treated. Nonetheless, the position that such factors must be "constitutionally an irrelevance," . . . summed up by the shorthand phrase "[o]ur Constitution is colorblind." . . . has never been adopted by this Court as the proper meaning of the Equal Protection Clause. Indeed, we have expressly rejected this proposition on a number of occasions.[70]

Justice Blackmun, in his separate opinion, stated the connection to *Plessy* as clearly as it possibly could have been stated:

I suspect that it would be impossible to arrange an affirmative-action program in a racially neutral way and have it successful. To ask that this be so is to demand the impossible. In order to get beyond racism, we must first take account of race. There is no other way. And in order to treat some persons equally, we must treat them differently.[71]

Justice Blackmun could have used the word "separately" in lieu of "differently" without changing his meaning in the slightest. Many liberal constitutionalists have openly suggested that something like the "separate but equal" doctrine may be the necessary foundation of racial preferences. Lawrence Tribe, for example, has made this remarkable statement: "It remains true, however, that judicial rejection of the 'separate but equal' talisman seems to have been accompanied by a potentially troublesome lack of sympathy for racial separateness as a possible expression of group solidarity."[72] Tribe's tergiversations indicate that it is not yet entirely fashionable to speak openly about the desirability of returning to separate but equal. Attacks on the idea of a color-blind constitution, in contrast, are legion.

Justice Powell, despite his forceful arguments disallowing racial classifications under the equal protection clause, did argue that race was a legitimate factor in the University of California's admissions process, but only as an aspect of "academic freedom"—to facilitate the creation of a "diverse student body" to enhance the intellectual atmosphere.[73] The intrusion of race, Powell remarked, must be on an individual basis and not part of any consideration that establishes or amounts to racial class considerations. But academic freedom is a First Amendment freedom, and the university is unique in that it has First Amendment interests. Only four members of the Court in *Bakke* agreed that racial classifications were allowable under the equal protection clause.[74] The *Weber* case skirted the issue by proclaiming that no "state action" was involved in the affirmative action program there under consideration. Whatever equivocation the Court may have engaged in respecting Congress's intent in passing the Civil Rights Act Of 1964, it managed to avoid the question of race classifications under the Fourteenth Amendment. The decision in *Weber* did, however, effectively convert the Civil Rights Act into class legislation providing class remedies for class injuries. The majority maintained that a literal reading of the Civil Rights Act would defeat its real intention—which was "to permit" (the "expressly" omitted phrase in section 703[j] *voluntary* "race conscious affirmative action programs."[75]

Chief Justice Burger's plurality opinion in *Fullilove v. Klutznick* (1980) rested principally on Congress's spending power, the general welfare clause and the commerce clause. Burger did, however, make some rather expansion comments about the equal protection clause. *Fullilove* involved a challenge to the Minority Business Enterprise portion of the 1977 Public Works Employment Act, which provided a ten percent set-aside for minority businesses in local public works projects. The set-aside applied to blacks, Hispanics, Orientals, Indians, and Aleuts. Burger wrote:

> A review of our cases persuades us that the objectives of the MBE program are within the power of Congress under [section] 5 "to enforce by appropriate legislation" the equal protection guarantees of the Fourteenth Amendment.
>   In *Katzenbach v. Morgan* (1966), we equated the scope of this authority with the broad powers expressed in the Necessary and Proper Clause . . ."[76]

Thus it seems that Congress's power to make "benign" racial classifications is as broad as its powers under the necessary and proper clause. And, as Burger well knows, those powers are expansive, to say the least. Addressing the question of equity, Burger further remarked:

> It is not a constitutional defect in this program that it may disappoint the expectations of nonminority firms. When effectuating a limited and properly tailored remedy to cure the effects of prior discrimination, such "a sharing of the burden" by innocent parties is not impermissible [citing, *inter alia, United Jewish Organizations*]. The actual "burden" shouldered by nonminority firms is relatively light. . . . Moreover, although we may assume that the complaining parties are innocent of any discriminatory conduct, it was within congressional power to act on the assumption that in the past some nonminority businesses may have reaped competitive benefit over the years from the virtual exclusion of minority firms from these contracting opportunities.[77]

Burger thus maintains that injury to "innocent parties" is permissible when the injury is "relatively light." But as the Court once said, "[t]he degree of the discrimination is irrelevant."[78] Although it may be true that the burden is "bearable," it still militates against the principle of equal protection. And in constitutional government, principle is everything, for it is precisely adherence to principle that distinguishes constitutional government from other kinds of government.

Fullilove provoked a bitter dissent from Justice Stewart who wrote that "in the exercise of its powers, Congress must obey the Constitution. . . . The statute, on its face and in effect . . . bars the members of [a] class solely on the basis of their race or ethnic background. This is precisely the kind of law that the guarantee of equal protection forbids."[79] Stewart ended his dissent with the remark that "[t]here are those who think that we need a new Constitution, and their views may someday prevail. But under the Constitution we have, one practice in which government may never engage is the practice of racism—not even 'temporarily' and not even as an 'experiment.'"[80] Indeed, it is a rather ominous sign that *Fullilove* represents the first case to uphold a racial classification expressed on the face of the law since *Korematsu*.

In the years after *Fullilove,* the Court has exhibited considerable confusion in affirmative action cases, particularly the question of whether rights adhere to individuals or groups. In *Firefighters Local Union No. 1784 v. Stotts* (1984), the Court by a 5–4 majority shed some doubt on the use of classwide remedies under Title VII of the Civil Rights Act of 1964. Justice White, writing for the majority, stated that "mere membership in the disadvantaged class is insufficient . . . each individual must prove that the discriminatory practice had an impact on him."[81] Since Justice White had signed the "joint separate opinion" in *Bakke,* this decision seemed to signal an important new consensus on the Court. This proved to be illusory, however. Plurality opinions in *Wygant v. Jackson Board of Education* (1986) and *United States v. Paradise* (1987) agreed that "some elevated level of scrutiny is required when a racial or ethnic distinction is made for remedial purposes." But as the plurality opinion in *Paradise* lamented, the Court "has yet to reach consensus on the appropriate constitutional analysis."[82] The questions that remained outstanding were to what extent did the governmental agencies and courts who employed racial classifications to remedy discrimination or the present effects of past discrimination have to base their race conscious actions on a formal finding that the governmental entity had committed discriminatory acts in the past; and the degree to which racial class injuries could support classwide remedies.

In *City of Richmond v. Croson* (1989) a badly divided Court declared Richmond's minority set-aside program to be a violation of the equal protection clause. The city of Richmond, which has a fifty percent black population, passed an ordinance that required nonminority-owned prime contractors awarded city construction contracts to set-aside thirty percent of the dollar amount of the contract for one or more minority owned business enterprises from anywhere in the United States. The principal reason that the Court gave for its decision was that the finding of discrimination upon which the ordinance was premised was too generalized and that the resultant remedy was not narrowly tailored. As Justice O'Connor remarked, writing for a majority in this part of the decision, "[l]ike the 'role model' theory employed in *Wygant,* a generalized assertion that there has been past discrimination in an entire industry provided no guidance for a legislative body to determine the precise scope of the injury it seeks to remedy."[83] O'Connor went on to remark that "the mere recitation of a 'benign' or legitimate purpose for a racial classification, is entitled to little or no weight . . . The history of racial classification in this county suggests that blind judicial deference to legislative or executive pronouncements of necessity has no place in equal protection analysis."[84] Significantly Justice O'Connor cited Justice Murphy's *dissenting* opinion in *Korematsu* as authority for this statement! As Justice O'Connor concluded, "[t]o accept Richmond's claim that past societal discrimination alone can serve as the basis for rigid racial preferences would be to open the door to competing claims for 'remedial relief' for every disadvantaged group. The dream of a Nation of equal citizens in a society where race is irrelevant to personal opportunity and achievement would be lost in a mosaic of shifting preferences based on inherently unmeasurable claims of past wrongs . . . We think such a result would be contrary to both the letter and spirit of a constitutional provision whose central command is equality."[85] Indeed, there is simply no principled way to resolve such competing class claims in a manner consistent with the rule of law.

Justice Marshall, in a bitter dissent, remarked that "today's decision marks a deliberate and giant step backward in this Court's affirmative action jurisprudence" by requiring "adequate findings to prove . . . past discrimination."[86] Marshall would simply rely upon a generalized knowledge of discrimination to support racial preferences expressed on the face of the law. Whether Marshall's jurisprudence would represent progress in racial relations is a matter that is entirely open to dispute, however.

In a part of her decision not joined by a majority, Justice O'Connor tried to make the point that section five of the Fourteenth Amendment allowed only Congress to undertake programs to enforce its equal protection commands. She thus tried to distinguish *Fullilove*. But Justice Kennedy in his concurring opinion pointed out the defect of O'Connor's attempt to carve out a middle ground where none exists. "The process," Kennedy wrote, "by which a law that is an equal protection violation when enacted by a State becomes transformed to an equal protection guarantee when enacted by Congress poses a difficult proposition for me; but as it is not before us, any reconsideration of that issue must await some further case. . . . The moral imperative of racial neutrality is the driving force of the Equal Protection Clause."[87] The next case was *Metro Broadcasting, Inc. v. F.C.C.* (1990) and it was to find both Justice Kennedy and O'Connor on the same side—in dissent.

Metro Broadcasting produced a clear majority of five and was the last major opinion written by Justice Brennan before his retirement from the Court. At issue in *Metro* was the Federal Communications Commission's policy of giving racial and ethnic group preferences in the issuance of broadcast licenses. The purported goal of the preferential policy was to foster "broadcast diversity." Brennan indicated that the court would accord extraordinary deference to the Congress: "It is of overriding significance in these cases that the FCC's minority ownership programs have been specifically approved—indeed mandated—by Congress."[88] And, for the first time since *Korematsu,* a clear majority of the Court decided that the appropriate test for "racial classifications" was not strict scrutiny but the less demanding "important governmental interests test." As Justice Brennan remarked,

> [w]e hold that benign race-conscious measures mandated by Congress—even if those measures are not 'remedial' in the sense of being designed to compensate victims of past governmental or societal discrimination—are constitutionally permissible to the extent that they serve important governmental objectives within the power of Congress and are substantially related to achievement of those objectives.[89]

It was, of course, not entirely surprising that Brennan would further find that the FCC policy did meet both prongs of the important governmental interest test. The novelty of the holding in *Metro* is breathtaking. Racial classifications will no longer automatically trigger the most searching examination if they are purported to benefit members of preferred groups. What is more, there is no longer any necessity of justifying the classifications in terms of providing remedies for victims of discrimination. In fact, there was no necessity of demonstrating that preferential policies to encourage minority ownership would in fact lead to programming diversity. It is enough, Brennan wrote, that "both Congress and the FCC maintain simply that expanded minority ownership of broadcast outlets will, in the aggregate, result in greater broadcast diversity."[90] Assuming, *arguendo,* that "broadcast diversity" serves important governmental interests, there seems to be some doubt even in Brennan's mind that the means chosen by the FCC to promote diversity are substantially related to that interest. "While we are under no illusion," Brennan intoned, "that members of a particular minority group share some cohesive, collective viewpoint, we believe it a legitimate *inference* for Congress and the Commission to draw that as more minorities gain ownership and policymaking roles in the media, varying perspectives will be more fairly represented on the airwaves.[91] Assuming that members of racial or ethnic groups share the same opinions and viewpoints would, of course, partake of the kind of "impermissible stereotyping" disallowed by the equal protection clause. But as Justice O'Connor points out in her dissenting opinion, when the FCC wanted to undertake a study to determine whether the nexus between minority ownership and broadcast diversity existed in any significant sense, "Congress barred the FCC's attempt to initiate that examination" through its control over "appropriations measures."[92] Without a clear demonstration of that nexus, however, the race-conscious policy cannot be said to serve an important government interest. Racial classifications are thus merely based on assumptions and inferences. One does not have to be well steeped in the history of race relations to see the danger of such a frivolous policy.

Brennan concludes his majority opinion by rehearsing some leading justifications used by the proponents of racial consciousness. "Such a goal," he writes, "carries its own natural limit, for there will be need for further minority preferences once sufficient diversity has been achieved."[93] Yet it has been almost twenty-five years since the proponents of affirmative action assured a skeptical world that race conscious policies would be temporary. Instead, affirmative action has come to be looked upon as racial class entitlements. But, Brennan still assures us, these policies do not "impose impermissible burdens on nonminorities." Of course, "innocent persons may be called upon" to bear the burden of eradicating the present effects of past discrimination, a discrimination in which they played no role. This is all acceptable within the new universe of equal protection jurisprudence because policies such as those of the FCC do "not impose an *undue* burden on nonminorities."[94]

O'Connor begins her dissent with a statement that stands "[a]t the heart of the Constitution's guarantee of equal protection," the "simple command that the Government must treat citizens 'as *individuals,* not as simply components of a racial, religious, sexual or national class.'"[95] O'Connor rightly points out what was obvious to any adherent of traditional equal protection analysis: "The Constitution clearly prohibits allocating valuable goods such as broadcast licenses simply on the basis of race." In O'Connor's view, the attempt to imply a nexus between minority ownership and broadcast diversity was simply a pretext. The "repeated focus on ownership supports the inference that the FCC seeks to allocate licenses based on race, an impermissible end, rather than to increase diversity of viewpoints, the asserted interest."[96] In this instance, the majority has converted the equal protection component of the Fifth Amendment's due process clause into a protection for a racial spoils system. Actually, as Kennedy's dissent correctly points out, *Bolling v. Sharpe* (1954), the case that held Congress to the same equal protection standards as the states under the Fourteenth Amendment, was "in effect overruled today."[97]

This, of course, was implied throughout Brennan's majority opinion. It is true that a majority of the Court will no longer hold the federal government bound by equal protection guarantees, then the consequences are likely to be unbearable for nomminority and minorities alike. In Kennedy's view, not only does the majority opinion base itself on the "separate but equal" doctrine of *Plessy* but bears more unsettling undertones of racial apartheid as well. As Justice Kennedy well knows, when the genie of race is set loose once again across the land, there is no guarantee that it will work for "benign" rather than destructive purposes. Anyone who can seriously talk about "benign" racial discrimination or race-consciousness simply does not understand the fragile character of political life. As Kennedy reminded us, it is "the cardinal rule that our Constitution protects each citizen as an individual, not as a member of a group."[98] This is the only sure way to "get beyond racism."

The intrusion of class into the Constitution is a dangerous proposition, one that is clearly at odds with the principles of the regime—principles that are ultimately derived from the proposition that "all men are created equal." Class considerations explicitly deny this equality because they necessarily abstract from the individual and ascribe to him or her class characteristics that are different—and necessarily unequal—from those of individuals inhabiting other classes. If there were no inequalities implicit in class distinctions, such distinctions would simply be superfluous.

The Founders of the regime knew well that class politics, whatever its character, was incompatible with the moving principles of liberal government. Madison, for example, described the problem of republican constitutionalism in this manner: "It is of great importance in a republic, not only to guard the society against the oppression of its rulers; but to guard one part of the society against the injustice of the other part" (No. 51, 351). The first aspect of the problem is addressed by the separation of powers; the second, and more difficult problem, requires an extensive regime with a "multiplicity of interests" designed to mitigate against the formation of "majority faction." As noted in Chapter Two, in the structure of the regime, the Founders expected the struggle between interests to replace the struggle between classes. And, by and large, the solution of the Founders has worked remarkably well. There have been no permanent majorities, and certainly none based exclusively on race.

Nonetheless, Professor Ely in his influential *Democracy and Distrust* argues:

> We are a nation of minorities and our system thus depends on the ability and willingness of various groups to apprehend those overlapping interests that can bind them into a majority on a given issue; prejudice blinds us to overlapping interests that in fact exist. As Frank Goodman put it so well eight years ago: "Race prejudice divides groups that have much in common (blacks and poor whites) and unites groups (white, rich and poor) that have little else in common than their antagonism for the racial minority. Race prejudice, in short, provides the 'majority of the whole' with that 'common motive to invade the rights of other citizens' that Madison believed improbable in a pluralistic society."[99]

Ely points to no specific examples but, like the Court in its recent cases, assumes the existence of a "monolithic" white majority from which "discrete and insular minorities" are permanently excluded. But the kind of permanent white majority that Ely and a majority of the Court have manufactured has never existed in American politics, not even before the Civil War. Nevertheless, Ely would establish as a solution a modified version of Kant's categorical imperative, one that does not depend on its universality as a guarantee of justice, but one that rests on the positive disadvantage of the majority. He argues that only legislation that imposes *disadvantages* upon the majority should be constitutionally nonsuspect since only the imposition of such disadvantage precludes the possibility that legislation that on its face has no discriminatory purpose is really nondiscriminatory.[100]

Ely further argues that "the Fourteenth Amendment quite plainly imposes a judicially enforceable duty of virtual representation. . . ." for "disfavored minorities"—any group "we know to be the object of widespread vilification, groups we know others . . . *might wish* to injure."[101] Since, as Ely realizes, his modified Kantianism is not a practicable solution, the task of providing "virtual representation" devolves upon the Supreme Court, the least representative body, and for that reason the one most capable of providing the kind of virtual representation that Ely envisions. The Court's prime responsibility under the

Fourteenth Amendment will be protection of "discrete and insular" minorities against deprivations of not only their constitutional rights, but also their "constitutionally gratuitous" rights as well—that is, the protection of "benefits . . . goods, rights, exemptions, or whatever" from "malfunction in their distribution."[102] This requires that whatever is distributed must be distributed (or redistributed) equally. This argument of Ely's, while displaying a certain ingenuity, is not atypical of recent commentators who look to the Court as the vehicle for extending the bureaucratic welfare state, a state that will obviously no longer have the "consent of the governed" as the moving principle of its politics.

But Professor Ely is mistaken; the guarantee of justice does not rest on a test of who is disadvantaged and whether the disadvantage amounts to "stigma," but on whether the common good is served. The most obvious cases in point are the Civil Rights Act of 1964 and the Voting Rights Act of 1965. The singular fact to emerge from the election of 1960 was that the solid vote of urban blacks for Kennedy accounted for the narrow margin of victory over Nixon. Since this same urban vote had gone for Eisenhower in 1956, the evident political strategy for the Democrats in the 1960s was to consolidate this vote in the Democratic camp. The Civil Rights Act of 1964 and the Voting Rights Act of 1965, whatever altruism they may have displayed as remedies for "historic" discrimination, were a large part of the attempt to keep the urban black vote solidly Democratic. They were thus not laws intended to protect those who were "isolated from the majoritarian political process," but a recognition that blacks had become a significant and crucial part of the governing majority.[103] And this is not unlike the situation that led to the passage of the second section of the Fourteenth Amendment[104] and the Fifteenth Amendment. This is Madisonian politics at its best, creating a situation where it is in the interest of the majority to protect and extend the rights and interests of the minority. Probably no finer examples of legislation serving the common good in this respect can be found than the Civil Rights Act of 1964 and the Voting Rights Act of 1965. But treating these acts as class remedies for class injuries undermines the ground of the common good upon which they rest. Understanding American politics in terms of "monolithic" majorities and "discrete and insular minorities" precludes the possibility of ever creating a common interest or common ground that transcends racial class considerations. By transforming the Fourteenth Amendment into an instrument of class politics, the Court runs the considerable risk either of making a majority faction more likely as the majority inevitably becomes more aware of its class status as a majority, or of transforming the liberal regime into one no longer based on majority rule. It is no accident that much current scholarship is directed at undermining the legitimate authority of majority rule. But if majority rule is under attack, then so is the principle of the "consent of the governed," and with it the principle of equality.

NOTES

1   274 U.S. 200, 208 (1927).
2   Alexis de Tocqueville, *Democracy in America,* J. P. Mayer, ed. (New York: Doubleday, 1969), p. 538; see also p. 673.
3   304 U.S. 144 (1938).
4   See, e.g., Terrence Sandalow, "Judicial Protection of Minorities," 75 *Michigan Law Review* (1972), p. 1162: "Forty years later, that cautious suggestion has ripened into an attitude."
5   300 U.S. 379, 391 (1937).
6   George Braden, "The Search for Objectivity in Constitutional Law," 57 *Yale Law Journal* (1940), pp. 579–580.
7   *Carolene,* at 152.
8   Braden, at 580.
9   *Carolene,* at 152 n. 4.
10 319 U.S. 624, 638 (1943).
11 Milner Ball, "Judicial Protection of Powerless Minorities," 59 *Iowa Law Review* (1974), p. 1062.
12 See, e.g., Raoul Berger, *Government by Judiciary: The Transformation of the Fourteenth Amendment* (Cambridge: Harvard University Press, 1977), pp. 275–277; J. H. Ely, *Democracy and Distrust* (Cambridge: Harvard University Press, 1980), pp. 75–77; Louis Lusky, *By What Right? A Commentary on the Supreme Court's Power to Revise the Constitution* (Charlottesville, VA: Michie Co., 1975), p. 12; Braden, p. 580 n. 28; Lusky, "Minority Rights and the Public Interest, 52 *Yale Law Journal* (1942), pp. 20–21. Lusky, who was Stone's clerk, was the author of the first draft of the footnote; and in its original form it did not include paragraph one. It was added by Stone in response to Hughes's query whether, in respect to "discrete and insular minorities," the "considerations [were] different" or whether "the difference lie not in the *test,* but in the nature of the rights invoked." Those who object to the first paragraph argue that the Constitution guarantees exclusively procedural rights. Stone, however, seems to have viewed constitutional procedures as a *means* for securing constitutional rights." See Letter from H. F. Stone to C. E. Hughes (April 19, 1938), quoted in Alpheus Mason, *The Supreme Court: Palladium of Freedom* (Ann Arbor: University of Michigan Press, 1962), p. 155.
13 *Reynolds v. Sims,* 377 U.S. 533, 562 (1964) (quoting *Yick Wo. v. Hopkins,* 118 U.S. 356, 370 (1896)).
14 17 U.S. (4 Wheat.) 316, 428 (1819).
15 303 U.S. 177, 180 (1938).
16 Id. at 184.
17 Id. at 184 n. 2 (citations omitted).
18 Id. (citations omitted) (emphasis added).
19 Id. See also *Southern Pac. Co. v. Arizona,* 325 U.S. 761, 767 n. 2 (1945) (Stone, C. J.); *McGoldrick v. Berwind-White Coal Mining Co.,* 309 U.S. 33, 45 n. 2 (1940) (Stone, J.); *Helvering v. Gerhardt,* 304 U.S. 405, 416 (1938) (Stone, J.).
20 310 U.S. 586, 606 (1940) (Stone, J., dissenting) (emphasis added).

21 Id. at 603.

22 See supra note 12. Lusky seemed never to have become reconciled to the addition of paragraph one to the note. His intention—but evidently not Stone's—was to give precedence to procedural guarantees. In his 1942 article Lusky quoted the note without mentioning paragraph one, Lusky, supra note 26, at 20; and, in a bitter complaint about Hughes's opinion for a unanimous Court in *Brown v. Mississippi,* 297 U.S. 278 (1936), he remarked:

> [T]he Court had reversed three murder convictions based on confessions obtained through physical torture. There was nothing in the opinion to suggest that it made any difference whatever that the defendants were Negroes, on trial in the deep South for a crime of violence. . . . The reasoning proceeded in terms of *individual* rights, there being no suggestion that the particular injustice there complained of might be especially deserving of Federal cognizance because race prejudice rendered remote the possibility of corrective action through the local political process.

Lusky, "Minority Rights and the Public Interest," p. 26. See also Lusky, "Footnote Redux: A Carolene Products Reminiscence," 82 *Columbia Law Review* (1982), p. 1093.

23 336 U.S. 77, 90–91 (1949) (Frankfurter, J., concurring). See also Braden, supra note 6, at 581–582.

24 Alpheus Mason, *Harlan Fiske Stone: Pillar of the Law* (New York: Viking Press, 1956), p. 512.

25 See, e.g., *Braunfeld v. Brown,* 366 U.S. 599, 613 (1961) (Brennan, J., concurring and dissenting) (footnote four was "prescient").

26 See, e.g., *Thomas v. Collins,* 323 U.S. 516, 530 (1945); *AFL v. Swing,* 312 U.S. 321, 325 (1941); *Thornhill v. Alabama,* 3310 U.S. 88, 95 (1940).

27 400 U.S. 112, 295 n. 14 (Stewart, J., concurring in part and dissenting in part).

28 403 U.S. 1, 5 (1970).

29 403 U.S. 365, 372 (1971) (citations omitted).

30 See *Nyquist v. Mauclet,* 432 U.S. 1 (1977); *Examining Bd. of Eng'rs v. Otero,* 426 U.S. 572 (1976); *Hampton v. Mow Sun Wong,* 426 U.S. 88 (1976); *In re Griffiths,* 413 U.S. 717 (1973); *Sugarman v. Dougall,* 413 U.S. 634 (1973).

31 Although the Court has not accorded "discrete and insular" minority status to illegitimacy, it has said that classifications based on illegitimacy are subject to strict scrutiny. In *Mathews v. Lucas,* 427 U.S. 495, 506 (1976), the Court noted that "discrimination between individuals on the basis of their legitimacy does not 'command extraordinary protection from the majoritarian political process' . . . which our *most exacting scrutiny* would entail" (emphasis added). Thus we see that the scrutiny reserved for "discrete and insular" minorities is the most stringent, more so than "ordinary" strict scrutiny.

32 See *San Antonio Indep. School Dist. v. Rodriguez,* 411 U.S. 1 (1973). But see *Harper v. Virginia Bd. of Elections,* 383 U.S. 663, 668 (1966).

33 See *Johnson v. Robison,* 415 U.S. 361 (1974).

34 411 U.S. 1, 105 (1973) (Marshall, J., dissenting).

35 Id. at 109.

36 Id. at 28.

37 *Sugarman v. Dougall,* 413 U.S. 634, 657 (1973) (Rehnquist, J., dissenting).

Rehnquist's remark has proved prescient. In his 1979 Francis Biddle Memorial Lecture at Harvard, Judge J. Skelly Wright remarked:

> The potential sweep of the equal protection clause is now known to be much greater than was imagined by the framers of the fourteenth amendment. . . . [T]he equal protection clause is primarily concerned with classes or groups, not individuals. As I am confident Mr. Justice Frankfurter must have written somewhere, a case invoking the equal protection clause, if it is to succeed, must allege something more than a tort, personal to the plaintiff. Once that is appreciated, it is plain that the relative position of the affected group often will determine the degree, and the kind, of injury that results from particular action. I need not catalog all the variables; suffice it to note that political impotency, numerical minority, low economic status, "outcast" social standing, public unpopularity, a sense of insecurity, and lack of self-confidence are among them.

Skelly Wright, "Judicial Review and the Equal Protection Clause," 15 *Harvard Civil Rights-Civil Liberties Law Review* (1980), pp. 17, 27. Suffice it to say that on Judge Wright's terms when one completed the enumeration of all the classes, the "affected groups" would resolve themselves once again into individuals. See Edward Erler, "Equal Protection and Regime Principles," in Robert L. Utley, Jr., ed., *The Promise of American Politics* (Lanham, MD: University Press of America, 1989), pp. 276–277.

38 See Sandalow, supra note 4, at 1174: "The minority has not, typically, been excluded from the political process leading to enactment of the legislation. It has simply lost." See also Mark Tushnet, "Darkness on the Edge of Town: The Contributions of John Hart Ely to Constitutional Theory," 89 *Yale Law Journal* (1980), p. 1052; but as Professor Karst remarks, "[e]very loser in the legislative process is by definition a minority, and at least potentially classifiable as disadvantaged," although a "doctrinal escape" requires a distinction "between minorities that seem permanently 'voiceless and invisible' and those that do not." "This principle," Karst continues, "is the equal protection analogue of the double standard of judicial review under the due process clauses, enunciated in Justice Stone's footnote 4, which made the legitimacy of judicial protection of the losers in the legislative process turn on the losers' long-term chances of becoming winners." Kenneth Karst, "Invidious Discrimination: Justice Douglas the Return of the 'Natural-Law-Due-Process Formula'," 16 *U.C.L.A. Law Review* (1969), pp. 742–743.

39 438 U.S. 265, 289–290 (1978).

40 323 U.S. 214, 216 (1944).

41 Id. at 220.

42 See *Lindsley v. Natural Carbonic Gas Co.*, 220 U.S. 61, 78–79 (1911): "If any state of facts reasonably can be conceived that would sustain it, the existence of that state of facts at the time the law was enacted must be assumed. One who assails the classification in such a law must carry the burden of showing that it does not rest upon any reasonable basis, but is essentially arbitrary."

43 Gerald Gunther, "The Supreme Court, 1971 Term—Forward: In Search of Evolving Doctrine on a Changing Court: A Model for a Newer Equal Protection," 86 *Harvard Law Review* (1972), pp. 8, 17.

44 *Bakke,* at 295.

45 Id. at 298.

46 Id. at 400.

47 *Los Angeles Dept. of Water & Power v. Manhart,* 435 U.S. 702, 708 (1977).

48 Hadley Arkes, *The Philosopher in the City: The Moral Dimensions of Urban Politics* (Princeton, NJ: Princeton University Press, 1981), pp. 47–49, 242, 253.

49 1 *Pomeroy's Equity Jurisprudence,* par. 93, at 122 (5th ed., S. Symons, 1941).

50 *Bakke,* at 298.

51 Id. at 299 (citations omitted).

52 Id. at 298.

53 430 U.S. 144, 152 (opinion of White, J.).

54 Id. at 165.

55 Id. at 174 (Brennan, J., concurring in part).

56 Id. at 178 (Brennan, J., concurring in part).

57 *Peters v. Kiff,* 407 U.S. 493 (1972).

58 430 U.S. 482, 499–500 (1977).

59 Id. at 515 (Powell, J., dissenting).

60 Id. at 503 (Marshall, J., concurring).

61 *Bakke,* at 300.

62 See Edmund Kitch, "The Return of Color-Consciousness to the Constitution: Weber, Dayton, and Columbus," 1979 *Supreme Court Review* (1979), p. 11. According to Kitch, the Court proceeds

> with concepts of class liability and careful inattention to the critical and revealing question: How is the remedy related to the wrong? In *Weber,* young white workers must be accorded lower status because craft unions to which they never belonged, once, in a manner then thought legal, discriminated against blacks. . . . The methodology of the Court is to find unconstitutional but not necessarily malevolent acts on the part of a school official, a craft union, the society, and then order relief the adverse effects of which fall only on those—the young family, student, or worker—who have no demonstrable connection to the wrong being redressed. Meanwhile, the individuals responsible—the former school board officials, the former members of craft unions, the former members of the Court itself—remain unaffected, protected by the scope of their official immunities or the passage of time.

63 *Bakke,* at 362 (opinion of Brennan, White, Marshall, and Blackmun, JJ.) (emphasis added). "Nor has anyone suggested that the University's purposes contravenes the *cardinal principle* that racial classifications that stigmatize—because they are drawn on the presumption that one race is inferior to another or because they put the weight of government behind racial hatred and separatism—are invalid without more." Id. at 357–358 (emphasis added).

64 *Bakke,* at 357 (quoting *San Antonio Indep. School Dist. v. Rodriguez,* 411 U.S. 1, 28 (1973); and citing *United Sates v. Carolene Prods. Co.,* 304 U.S. 144, 152 n. 4 (1938). See also *Fullilove v. Klutznick,* 448 U.S. 448, 518 (1980) (Marshall, J., concurring).

65 163 U.S. 537, 559 (1896) (Harlan, J., dissenting).

66 *Brown v. Board of Education,* 347 U.S. 483, 494–495 (1954).

67 *Plessy,* at 551.

68 *Brown,* at 495 (emphasis added).

69 *Bakke,* at 336.

70 Id. at 355–356. Among the cases cited as the authority for this interpretation is

Korematsu. Scholars have only belatedly "discovered" that the ideal of a colorblind constitution is, at bottom, only a "myth." In fact, it has been argued that colorblindness, insofar as it has reference to race, is itself a race-conscious idea—and can therefore be used to justify "benign" racial discrimination. See David Strauss, "The Myth of Colorblindness," 1986 *Supreme Court Review* 99–134 (1986).

71 Id. at 407 (opinion of Blackmun, J.).

72 L. Tribe, *American Constitutional Law,* 2nd ed. (Mineola, NY: Foundation Press, 1988), p. 1479.

73 *Bakke,* at 311–315 (opinion of Powell, J.).

74 Many observers, including, it seems, the Supreme Court, have misunderstood the limited scope of Powell's opinion with respect to the consideration of race as an aspect of academic freedom. Powell emphatically disallows considerations of race under the equal protection clause. See *Minnick v. California Dept. of Corrections,* 452 U.S. 105, 115–116 (1981).

75 See Kitsch, supra note 62, at 4:

The court argues that the absence of the phrase "require or permit" means that the statute does permit but not require. Mr. Justice Rehnquist points out the lack of force in this argument. Since there was no reason to believe that the statute did not interdict such preferential treatment outside the context of a remedy to correct a statutory violation, there was no reason for the Congress to provide that it would not permit what it did not permit.

One acute observer has also noted that "[i]f the definition of voluntary action used in [*Weber*] were applied to criminal confessions, it would be possible to condone torture." Barbara Lerner, "Employment Discrimination: Adverse Impact, Validity, and Equality," 1979 *Supreme Court Review* (1979) p. 45 n. 84.

76 448 U.S. 448, 476 (1980).

77 Id. at 484–485.

78 *Harper v. Virginia State Bd. of Elections,* 383 U.S. 663, 668 (1966).

79 *Fullilove,* at 526–527 (Stewart, J., dissenting).

80 Id. at 532.

81 467 U.S. 561, 579 (1984).

82 *United States v. Paradise,* 480 U.S. 149, 166 (1987).

83 109 S.Ct. 706, 723 (1989).

84 Id. at 725.

85 Id. at 727.

86 Id. at 740.

87 Id. at 734.

88 110 S.Ct. 2997, 3008 (1990).

89 Id. at 3008–3009.

90 Id. at 3016.

91 Id. at 3018 (emphasis added).

92 Id. at 3042 (O'Connor, J., dissenting).

93 Id. at 3025.

94 Id. at 3026 (emphasis original).

 95 Id. at 3028 (quoting *Arizona Governing Committee v. Norris,* 463 U.S. 1073, 1083 [1983]).

 96 Id. at 3041.

 97 Id. at 3045 (Kennedy, J., dissenting).

 98 Id. at 3046.

 99 J. H. Ely, *Democracy and Distrust,* p. 153.

100 Id. at 170–171.

101 Id. at 86, 153 (emphasis added).

102 Id. at 136.

103 Id. at 161; see C. Brauer, *John F. Kennedy and the Second Reconstruction* (New York: Columbia University Press, 1977), pp. 8, 38, 57–60, 273, 279.

104 See R. Berger, *Government By Judiciary,* pp. 176, 52, 70; J. James, *The Framing of the Fourteenth Amendment* (Urbana: University of Illinois Press, 1965), pp. 22, 46, 129–130, 180, 184.

Index

About the Author

Edward J. Erler is Professor of Political Science and Chair of the Department at California State University, San Bernardino. He has published extensively in the areas of constitutional law and political theory.